John Dewey,
Confucius,
and
Global Philosophy

SUNY series in Chinese Philosophy and Culture
Roger T. Ames, editor

John Dewey, Confucius, and Global Philosophy

Joseph Grange

Foreword by Roger T. Ames

STATE UNIVERSITY OF NEW YORK PRESS

Published by
State University of New York Press, Albany

Printed in the United States of America

For information, address State University of New York Press,
194 Washington Avenue, Suite 305, Albany, NY 12210-2384

Production by Judith Block
Marketing by Michael Campochiaro

Library of Congress Cataloging-in-Publication Data

Grange, Joseph, 1940–
   John Dewey, Confucius, and global philosophy / Joseph Grange ;
foreword by Roger T. Ames.
      p. cm. — (SUNY series in Chinese philosophy and culture)
   Includes bibliographical references (p.   ) and index.
   ISBN 0-7914-6115-7 (hardcover: alk. paper) — ISBN 0-7914-6116-5
(pbk. : alk. paper)
   1. Dewey, John, 1859–1952. 2. Confucius. 3. Philosophy, Comparative.
I. Title. II. Series.

B945.D44G72 2004
109'.2—dc22
                                                            2003061032

10 9 8 7 6 5 4 3 2 1

In Memory of David Hall
Master of Eros and Irony

Contents

Foreword

Roger T. Ames

As Joseph Grange insists throughout this present essay, in pursuing cultural understanding and accommodation between American and Chinese cultural sensibilities, there is quite simply no intelligent alternative to dialogue. And a dialogue to be meaningful requires a shared ground—an appreciation of continuities and differences revealed through an exploration of an overlapping cultural vocabulary. Grange draws upon his sustained and substantial reading of the original reflections of John Dewey and of Confucius to bring into focus several seminal ideas from each of these two traditions that provide us with a resonance between them, and that can serve us as the terms of art necessary for undertaking such a Sino-American dialogue.

To set the context for Grange's proposed cultural conversation, we might begin by asking the synoptic question: what, after all, do we mean by "Confucianism" and "Deweyan pragmatism?" It is only in coming to terms with this question that we are able to make the important connection between Grange's impassioned plea for a better world, and the vision for addressing such a task provided in the works of Confucius and Dewey.

Elsewhere I have argued for a *narrative* rather than an *analytical* understanding of Confucianism.[1] In short, framing the question as "What is Confucianism?" in analytical terms tends to essentialize Confucianism as a specific ideology—a technical philosophy—that can be stipulated with varying degrees of detail and accuracy. *What* is a question that is perhaps more successfully directed at attempts at systematic philosophy where through analysis one can seek to abstract the formal, cognitive structure in the language of principles, theories, and concepts. However, in evaluating the content and worth of a fundamentally aesthetic tradition that takes as its basic premise the uniqueness of each and every situation, and in which the goal of ritualized living is to redirect attention back to the level of concrete feeling, the *what* question is at best a first step. Beyond the *what* question, we need to ask more importantly after method: *how* has Confucianism functioned historically within the specific conditions of an evolving Chinese culture to try to make the most of its circumstances?

However we might choose to characterize Confucianism, it is more than any particular set of precepts or potted ideology identified post hoc within different phases or epochs of China's cultural narrative. Confucianism is not as much an isolatable doctrine or a commitment to a certain belief structure as it is the continuing narrative of a community of people—the center of an ongoing way or *dao* of thinking and living. Approaching the story of Confucianism as a continuing cultural narrative presents us with a rolling, continuous, and always contingent tradition out of which emerges its own values and its own logic. A narrative understanding of Confucianism is made available to us by drawing relevant correlations among specific historical figures and events. Confucianism is importantly biographical and genealogical—the stories of formative models. And in reflecting on the lives of Chinese *philosophes*—a survey of often passionate, sometimes courageous intellectuals who as heirs to the tradition of the "scholar-official" (*shi*) advance their own programs of human values and social order— we become immediately aware that any account of the existential, practical, and resolutely historical nature of this tradition makes it more (and certainly less) than what would be defined as "philosophers" doing philosophy within the contemporary Western context.

If we take Dewey on his own terms, the same distinction between narrative and analysis—method and ideology—might be directed at the question, "What is Deweyan pragmatism?" Robert Westbrook recounts how the early critics of pragmatism attacked it condescendingly as a "would-be philosophical system" with distinctively American characteristics, and how Dewey responded by readily allowing the relationship between philosophical ideas and the cultural sensibilities within which they are embedded.[2] The American sensibility is not to be found in an assessment of notions such as "fundamental principles," "system of values," "ruling theories," or "core beliefs." The term "sensibility" is best understood dispositionally as a nuanced manner of anticipating, responding to, and shaping the world about us. Sensibilities are complexes of *habits* that both create and are created by *habitats* and that promote specific, personal manners of *in-habiting* a world. Cultural sensibilities are not easily expressed through the analysis of social, economic, or even political institutions. Such sensibilities reside in the prominent feelings, ideas, and beliefs defining the culture.³ Richard Rorty certainly reminds us that while our American sensibility may be characterized partly through the description and analysis of ideas, it is perhaps most readily available through the indirection and evocation associated with poetry and literature.

At a personal level, the philosopher Dewey was a lifelong advocate of democracy, where his understanding of democracy was nothing more or less than the advocacy of a spiritual way of living that is described herein as "consummatory experience." Democracy is the flourishing community as it emerges concretely and processively through the equality and individuality of its specific members. In this respect, Dewey's long career as a social activist, taking him from the underbelly of Chicago to a simmering revolution in China to educational reform in Turkey to the Trotsky trials in Mexico City, was fair demonstration of his commitment to what in fact he called "the recovery of philosophy": "Philosophy recovers itself when it ceases to be a device for dealing with the problems of philosophers and becomes a method, cultivated by philosophers, for dealing with the problems of men."⁴

In the Confucian tradition too, philosophical "knowing" (*zhi*), far from being some privileged access to a Reality lying behind the everyday world, is an attempt to "realize" a world in the sense of orchestrating the existing conditions to make a desirable world real. Speaking in the broadest terms, Confucianism is a meliorative aestheticism concerned with appreciating the world—as Grange says, adding value to it—through the cultivation of a meaningful, communicating, human community. And the prominence of ritual as a primary level of communication in this process suggests that the site of realizing this world is ritualized, concrete feeling. In general terms, we can observe that the self-understanding of many Chinese philosophers approximates Dewey's vision of the philosopher as the purveyor of considered, intelligent practice to adjust situations and improve upon the human experience.

In exploring some of the more specific Deweyan vocabulary of consummatory experience below—concepts captured in the language of "experience," "felt intelligence," and "culture"—Grange provides us with a framework for recovering the insistent historical particularity that provides concrete exemplification of Dewey's own personal growth and articulation. In the case of Confucius, he is certainly "the Sage." However, he is best remembered by history not only through the episodes of his life depicted in the *Analects*, but also dispositionally by the specific personal habits as they are recounted in the middle books of this same text. For Dewey too, his own life experience and the cultivated habits of his heart and mind are perhaps the best measure of his philosophical profundity. It is no accident that the most sophisticated representations of his ideas are to be found in the philosophical biographies of interpreters such as Steven Rockefeller[5] and Westbrook.

It is entirely appropriate too that Joe Grange has chosen to dedicate this book to our mutual friend, David Hall, who in his own life understood and acted upon much that has been said here of Dewey and Confucius. For David, Deweyan pragmatism and Confucianism could both be fairly captured in the simple and yet profound challenge to become our own best thoughts.

Preface

The constant task of . . . thought is to establish working
connections between old and new subject-matters. . . .
[T]he greater the gap . . . the greater is the burden imposed
upon reflection; the distance between old and new is the
measure of the range and depth of the thought required.
                    —John Dewey, *Experience and Nature*

It is April 2001 as I write this preface and the words ricochet off the
walls: "Apologize, regret, sorry, very sorry." China and the United
States are literally in a war of words that threatens to become something else. Jets and spy planes and world peace hang on the nuance of
a word. How did it come to this? This book suggests an answer.

The roots of this crisis are to be found in the cultural meanings
by which these two global powers live. This is not the first time the
threat of violence has emerged from misunderstanding nor will it be
the last. What makes this situation important is that it so clearly marks
out the cultural sources of this and future disputes. The dispute centers
on the difference between "sorry" and "very sorry." For want of a
"very," the world could be very different today.

It is meanings that are at the root of this and other problems of
globalization. Is there a way to span this division and bring these two
powerful cultures into fruitful contact? Philosophy can be understood
as the critic of cultures. Culture rests on meanings. These meanings are
embedded in a nest of cultural presuppositions. Getting at these
cultural assumptions is the most difficult aspect of coaxing different
cultures to some level of mutual understanding.

I was therefore completely surprised when my graduate seminar on the philosophy of John Dewey given at the University of Hawaii in the late 1990s was so enthusiastically received by students of Asian descent and by students studying Chinese philosophy and culture. In fact Roger Ames, director of the Institute for Chinese Studies, attended these sessions and noted the similarity between Dewey's thought and Confucian philosophy. He asked if he could use a transcript of the seminar in his own course on human rights in China and the West. That experience was also favorable. So this book is the result of many hands. What I have tried to do is point out as simply and clearly as possible what I take to be the parallel understandings of culture and the human person found in the works of John Dewey and Confucius.

Hawaii is the midpoint of the Pacific poised to be the fulcrum around which future dialogue with Asia will occur. I saw that future as caught up in yet another question: what did Dewey share with Asia?

The plot thickened when I recalled that Dewey had spent sixteen months lecturing in China. Now as the recent problems over language clearly demonstrate, the Chinese are a very serious people. Therefore when I learned that the National University of China granted Dewey an honorary degree with a citation calling him a "Second Confucius," my ears pricked up. The Chinese are not flatterers given to easy compliments and to yoke this twentieth century philosopher with the founder of their cultural outlook is a matter of immense importance.

In creating this work I have tried to write in a clear down-to-earth style. Also I have deliberately created a short book, one that can quickly steer the reader toward what is important. To present in a clear way the insights of a great thinker is no easy task. And the difficulty is doubled when two thinkers are involved. Still: the way toward an adequate understanding remains open if a simple commandment is obeyed. A comparative philosopher's golden rule ought always be: stick to what is central. Therefore: the themes presented in this volume have been narrowed down to a select few: experience, felt intelligence, and culture. These ideas are radically transformed in the hands of John Dewey and Confucius. By the time this study is completed, they will have taken on fresh meanings. Hopefully, this transformation will help create deeper cultural understanding in an increasingly interconnected world.

My method is straightforward. In discussing these themes, I will first let Dewey have his say and then reengage his notion through a discussion of similar ideas in Confucian philosophy.[1] The result should be a set of interlocking ideas that take on thicker and deeper significance as the study proceeds. My aim is to present these interwoven themes as a support system for a cross-cultural dialogue on global understanding. If they are to serve their primary purpose, these ideas should exhibit two characteristics. First, they should be coherent in the sense that each theme requires a necessary reference to the others. This is one of the hallmarks of systematic philosophy as practiced in the West. It finds its analog in the Chinese insistence on the radical importance of conceptual polarity as the ground of thinking. Thus the yin-yang quality of Chinese thinking is matched by the demand for coherence in systematic thinking. Another quality shared by Dewey and Confucius is the need for direct experiential contact between the ideas offered and the actual world of human beings. Thoughts should make a difference. If they do not, they are empty and vain. The difference made by good thinking is to be found in the depth provided by the mixing of ideas and experience. Real ideas provide new dimensions that illuminate the situations within which we exist. Thus philosophy is always a form of cultural criticism. It should, as Dewey insisted, be directed towards the real problems of human beings rather than the problems of other professional philosophers.

The goal of this study is to provide a set of ideas so braided together that they provide a powerful new sense of the possibilities of human life. Both Dewey and Confucius share a similar conviction: human beings must grow in order to become fully human. They are not naturally good or bad. In fact, before their entrance into the social order, little can be said about who or what they are. There is therefore a primary dimension always to be taken into account whenever we talk about human culture. The social aspect is front and center when we speak of the possibilities of genuine human growth and development. To pretend that we are isolated individuals runs counter to our experience. Confucius and Dewey affirm the fact that to be human is *to live together*.

Sharing through association with others is what provides the depth necessary to recast our lives and alter our perspectives. Transformation is the mandate governing human life. This drive towards change is powerfully built up by our contacts with others. The quality and frequency of those associations will determine the level of human excellence we are able to attain. Our humanity is not given to us at birth. It must be earned and it is the responsibility of social orders to form the character of their members. This is why Confucius was so insistent upon the importance of developing a corps of scholar-officials to seed Chinese social and cultural life. It is also why experience, inquiry, and culture form the background of Dewey's critique of American culture.[2]

As is well known, Dewey insists on the importance of direct experience as the ultimate transformative agent. It is less well known that Confucius held a similar doctrine. The art of being human grows in direct proportion to our capacity to feel concretely the effects of our words and deeds. What we undergo and what we undertake has direct bearing on the temper of our personalities and the values that we hold. We change only to the extent that we can experience our values as constructive, deficient, appropriate or destructive.

Dewey and Confucius were fully aware of the dangers that lurked in the world of experience. Finding good outcomes is therefore an essential dimension of cultural development. It is through inquiry that satisfactory results are identified and experienced. Once again, what is meant by inquiry is far different from naive questioning or the adoption of sophisticated scientific methodologies. Investigating the structure and results of experience requires much more than the crude tools that we now use to determine the value of experience. Inquiry becomes a demanding affair that calls on every human power to determine and articulate what is really going on. What seems transparently easy turns out to be an exceptionally complex affair. This is why I substitute the phrase "felt intelligence" for the Dewey's customary term, "inquiry."

Sharing these findings and making them real for other human beings is a skill that needs constant retooling. A growing human culture requires an array of such tools. The arts are not mere cultural window dressing. They are the vital forces that weave together the shared meanings that mark a thriving culture. One must be able to make others feel what is happening before one analyzes the reasons why it is happening. A certain anesthesia creeps over societies when they are in decline. What becomes seriously enfeebled is the capacity to connect with what is going on. My opening remarks on words and bullets serve as a concrete example of how easy it is to mistake the meaning of others.

There is another negative outcome of the failure to communicate adequately the feel of a situation and the meaning of experience. I call it "the Rise of the Great Disconnect." Our culture is characterized by a startling number of disconnects between our lives and our experience. There is no flow between what we do, what we experience, and what we say. Other ages called it alienation, but Dewey's philosophy lets us name it more directly and precisely. We are plagued by a series of separations that run from our body through our mind and spirit and then through our social order. Each split prevents our experience from becoming whole and continuous. This series of disconnects prevents our lives from building up a fund of energy and value with which to face our future and respect our past. We live in a series of "nows" that may give momentary satisfaction but ultimately prevent us from seeing our lives as whole, as connected with others and as grounded in the meanings derived from shared experience. These disconnects form the basis of our impoverished lives. For despite the great material wealth generated by Western culture, we lack a sense of genuine achievement and inner peace. The effects of the Great Disconnect echo through this book. For is it not remarkable that, despite our material success, more and more citizens of the West "go East" to locate the things that nourish the soul? It is time that serious efforts be made to bridge the gap between so-called Asian Values and Western social and political accomplishments. This study is one contribution to that project.

Any one who has watched television for an extended period of time senses this loss of intensity. Our feelings become habituated to the programs that go forward for twelve minutes and then pause and promise to return (after these messages) with more insipid activities. Of course, the networks are acutely aware of losing their audience so they regularly employ the two most powerful agents for engaging human attention—sex and violence! Similarly, what should be one of the finest hours of communication, democracy, inquiry and experience (the political talk show)—degenerates into a food fight between nincompoops. One must also mention the truncated version of discourse that has come to dominate the world of the Internet and e-mail. But the point has been made. Western culture is at a crisis stage. It seems that the only achievement our culture can fall back on is our immense material wealth. But this accomplishment—seen in the light of the evils brought about by free market capitalism—loses its luster. And, finally, even our technological advances and medical breakthroughs are beginning to show their problematic side.

John Dewey is America's most distinguished philosopher. Confucian tradition runs throughout Asia. In bringing together these eminent cultural spokesmen, a way of living may be marked out that can reverse the downward spiral now infecting our increasingly globalized culture. Such is the hope of this essay in comparative philosophy. We need to seek and then use the "working connections" between these cultures.

I dedicate this book to the memory of David L. Hall, master of eros and irony and groundbreaking comparative philosopher. His genius has been a direct influence on my work. More than that, as a great friend, he has inspired me to do my best work. The world of philosophy has suffered a great loss with his untimely death. I also wish to acknowledge the help of Roger Ames, who urged me to write this book. Robert Neville and Chung-ying Cheng have also been trustworthy guides through the thickets of comparative philosophy. Linyu Gu has graciously supplied the Chinese glossary. Then there are the members of my Dewey seminar at the University of Hawaii, especially James Behuniak and Sor-hoon Tan, both of whom will soon be making important contributions to the growing field of Asian-American philosophy. There is also Yuri Van Mierlo, whose remarkable growth as a person and a ball player is celebrated later in this book. I am also grateful for the kindnesses of Anya and Robin. Finally, I thank Claudine for her patient love during the times this book was being written.

1

Experience

Dewey's Novel Insight

"Experience" is one of the most common words in our vocabulary. We say someone is experienced or we comment on how someone needs further experience. It is often used as a positive term and frequently connotes wisdom, superior skill and even a virtuous quality. As we say "Let's give this task to a very experienced person." Furthermore, we equate experience with learning and the ability to cope with many different and difficult situations. Conversely, lack of experience is regarded as a drawback and something to be overcome. So there is a general agreement that experience is a good, even a valuable quality.

So why is it that when Dewey began using the term to describe the centerpiece of his philosophy, so many professional philosophers went out of their way to lambaste him for destroying all that philosophy had achieved over the centuries? To many of his colleagues it appeared that Dewey had sold out to the man in street. He was seen as a crude popularizer and a mouthpiece for the worst sort of American materialism.

But this vicious criticism is also evidence that Dewey had touched a raw nerve in the groves of academic philosophy. By the time Dewey had reached a preeminent position in philosophy's professional hierarchy, another style of philosophizing was gaining recognition. It sought to purify philosophy of concerns with the problems of everyday life. Academic philosophy began to ape the sciences with their concern for exactness and absolute certainty. Epistemology, logic, philosophy of science, and verification procedures replaced debates about experience, inquiry, and culture. Variously called analytic philosophy or positivism, these schools had traded in their street clothes for the pure white lab coats favored by the sciences. Matters that mean the most to human beings took a back seat to abstract ruminations far removed from the problems of men and women. This "New Philosophy" was largely an import from Anglo-European schools of thought. It was almost totally unaware of the rich tradition of classical American philosophy. Thinkers like Royce, James, Peirce, and Dewey were scorned for their lack of sophistication. The fact that there was a thriving indigenous American philosophy rooted in its own soil and grappling with its own cultural problems escaped the notice of these "new" thinkers.

Such a valuable retrieval of our philosophical past can be gained by understanding why Dewey chose experience as the touchstone of his philosophy of culture. It also sets the stage for understanding the remarkable similarity between Dewey and Confucius. Both philosophers seek a category that can embrace in the widest possible terms the richest view of human existence. Dewey calls it experience. Confucius calls his fundamental category, "the Way" or "the *Dao*." It, too, depends upon the act of undergoing experience.

I will begin by describing what Dewey means by experience. Then we will be in a position to see how emphatically the ancient Chinese sage Confucius underscores the cultural philosophy of the modern American philosopher. What will result is a vital working connection that can serve as a tool for future efforts to understand the issues that divide China and America. What follows revolves about the meaning of value and the terms of its achievement.

The reconstruction of the idea of experience remains Dewey's enduring contribution to philosophy. One reason for this is the fact that Dewey was never afraid to send his thoughts out into the streets and see how they fared. And his account of experience continues to repay those who seek to understand it. His distinctive use of the term also distinguishes his way of doing philosophy from other philosophies. Experience became for him what the Forms were for Plato, Substance for Aristotle, and the "I think, therefore I am" for Descartes. And he employed it with the same sense of rigor that Kant used his A Priori, and Hegel his Dialectic. To understand Dewey's concept of experience is therefore to head straight for the heart of his philosophy.

A good place to begin would be with Dewey's own personal experiences with experience. In his early life, he tells us, he suffered from "inward lacerations of the spirit" brought on by the conflicts he underwent while growing from boyhood to manhood.[1] A laceration is a cut that causes deep fissures in the skin. It divides a naturally seamless surface into separated parts. These moments of alienation weighed heavily on Dewey, for he experienced them as conflicts keeping him from a wholehearted life. One finds the same sense of separation in the early writings of Dewey, where he struggles with the giants of European philosophy (Locke, Hume, Kant, and Hegel). A great interior clash goes on inside Dewey as he seeks to record his respect for these thinkers but also point out their limitations. And whether the thinkers are Kant and Hegel or the issues those of psychology or science, the enemy is always the same: *separations that make it impossible to feel, think, judge, will, or act as a whole human being.* What bothered Dewey most was the fact that the discipline traditionally charged with presenting an integrated view of nature, human beings, and the universe was guilty of devising ways and means to separate these interrelated domains. Philosophy had become the enemy of experience, not its champion.

But what is experience? We speak of good experiences and bad ones. We talk about something being "an experience" and we also say someone needs experience or lacks experience or even has to gain more experience. It appears to be quantitative as well as qualitative. It has an ethical edge to it and also some kind of transformative power. It teaches us and can also damage us. It can shock us and it can reassure us. It can lead us into strange new lands and it can frustrate our most cherished plans. It appears to be the most common of activities and at the same time the most mysterious. It seems to be everywhere in our lives; yet, when we seek to specifically locate it, it is nowhere to be found. It happens in space and in time but it also transforms these fundamental backdrops of experience. Without it human life would not be as we know it. At the same time it can not simply be reduced to human life itself. Neither is it the same as culture, although culture does depend on it. It changes its forms and expressions but also maintains a fundamental structure throughout all its appearances. It begins, it develops, and it comes to an end. But it is then succeeded by other experiences. It has unvarying elements but also registers its presence in varying ways. It is richly attuned to the situation within which it is had and at the same time, it can profoundly alter that situation.

Experience happens. This is the most important thing to know about it. It occurs. It is therefore an event and not a thing. All the categories we normally use to define things are not helpful here. In fact, they tend to lead us away from the meaning of experience. We can wrap our hands around a stone and we can focus our minds on an idea. But having an experience is something quite different from those activities. Experience happens as an experience. It brings itself about.

Where does experience happen? It always happens within a context or situation. To be more precise, experience happens within a field of other experiences. To express this aspect of experience I will say that experience always happens within a specific environment. It is partly dependent on and partly creative of the context within which it finds itself. A beaver finds itself in an environment within which it needs a stable supply of water. In building its dam, it alters its environmental field and thereby transforms its own experience as well as those of others connected to this particular region (for example, the fish, birds, plants, and insects that share the ecology of the region). But it does this not by changing these other beings but by transforming the field within which they and it live. These other beings are forced to react to these new conditions. They do this through their own experience.

Experience has many different elements. These components can come from the side of the experience or the environment itself. Whatever the origin, the complexity of experience should warn us against the very natural tendency to look for easy and simple answers to the question of experience. Even at this rudimentary level of analysis, we are already talking about an event that incorporates into its being a wide variety of different factors. In its drive to organize its world the beaver continually encounters what is different from itself. The tree it gnaws on. The bark it strips. The water it must hold back. Just how well it deals with these and other environmental elements will prove the merits of its experience.

This side of experience deals with the unfamiliar and therefore it has clinging to it an element of strangeness. This foreign feeling attached to the very beginnings of experience is significant. It provides a clue as to why experience is so powerful a force in our lives. Without it we would never encounter anything new or creative. It also tells us why so many humans are deathly afraid of experience. It invites the different into our lives and by unsettling our beliefs, changes our habits of being. Encountering the different is one hallmark of experience.

Every experience is also individual. The individuality of an experience derives from the ways in which it draws together the relations that make up its texture. Its way of dealing with the unfamiliar is unique to itself. Dewey sees each and every experience as a creative act introducing new ways of bringing harmony into the world. It is the special weaving introduced by each experience that deepens the value of the world.

It is for this reason that Dewey always associates experience with both *doing* and *undergoing*. Confronted with a situation, the act of experience always entails a double effort on the part of those involved. On the one hand, there is effort and strain as the situation is confronted and modes of action are undertaken in order to deal with it. We set out to correct an imbalance. This means we must devise schemes to bring about equilibrium. At the same time this effort meets resistance as we discover just how recalcitrant the world can be. We then undergo the push and pull of the world and encounter in the most concrete ways the otherness of the universe. We are part of nature, not all of it. This is when true learning and development begins. Experience is the teacher of the double fact of the need for effort and the need to suffer.

This is also the heart and soul of the transformative dimension of experience. It acts through direct engagement with the world. It is also why Dewey came to see it as the most important feature of a wise way of living. It unites thought and action, thinking and doing *naturally*. For Dewey came to see (largely under the influence of Darwin) how all of nature was a matter of experience. Every aspect of the natural world is involved in some form of experience—that is to say, some form of doing and undergoing. Each step in evolution is the outcome of learned responses to environmental experiences. Each shift in anatomy is the result of doing and undergoing in patterns of continuous experience. There is in other words an instrumental purpose embodied in experience. It has a built-in intelligence by reason of the factors of doing and undergoing. Natural beings learn about themselves through experience. Experience for Dewey is the medium within which we act. And as we engage it, we become more and more immersed in its intricate dance:

Experience is primarily a process of undergoing: a process of standing something, of suffering and passion, of affection, in the literal sense of these words. The organism has to endure, to undergo the consequences of its own actions. Experience is no slipping along in a path fixed by inner consciousness. Private consciousness is an incidental outcome of a vital objective sort; it is not its source. Undergoing, however, is never mere passivity. The most patient patient is more than a receptor. He is also an agent—a reactor, one trying experiments, one concerned with undergoing what is still to happen. Sheer endurance, side-stepping evasions, are, after all, ways of treating the environment with a view to what such treatment will accomplish. Even if we shut ourselves up in the most clam-like fashion, we are doing something; our passivity is an active attitude, not an extinction of response. Just as there is no assertive action, no aggressive attack upon things as they are, which is all action, so there is no undergoing which is not on our part also a going on and a going through.[2]

Within the push and pull of experience we find the reason why Dewey insists on the double features of experience, doing and undergoing. Experience works both ways. It shapes the environment within which it works and in turn it shapes the one undergoing the experience. This is experience's interactive side. It constitutes the engaged quality always to be found within the contours of genuine experience. Experience is an active presence in the world that makes a real difference in both the field within which it occurs and the one undergoing the experience. This means that the presence of resistance within an experience is a sign of the need for more intelligence in the process of doing and undergoing. We learn from experience because we are not totally in charge of the results of any authentic experience. Genuine experience is the best antidote for the narcissism that poisons our culture.

This interactive dimension demands that the push and pull of experience undergo continuous interpretation. To interpret is to locate the meanings that reside within an experience. Therefore, experience is always oriented toward questions of value. At its center there exists a demand for an interpretation of the values resident within its boundaries. There is no such thing as bare, empty experience. Something of value happens. Either experience makes a difference or it is not an experience. Therefore, to experience authentically is to undergo a profound transformation due to the interpretive imperative built into its heart:

> [T]he gist of the matter is that the immediate existence of quality, and of dominant and pervasive quality, is the background, the point of departure, and the regulative principle of all thinking. Thought which

denies the existential reality of qualitative things is therefore bound to end in self-contradiction and in denying itself. "Scientific" thinking, that expressed in physical science, never gets away from qualitative existence. Directly, it always has its own qualitative background; indirectly, it has that of the world in which the ordinary experience of the common man is lived. Failure to recognize this fact is the source of a large part of the artificial problems and fallacies that infect our theory of knowledge and our metaphysics, or theories of existence. With this general conclusion goes another that has been emphasized in the preceding discussion. Construction that is artistic is as much a case of genuine thought as that expressed in scientific and philosophical matters, and so is all genuine aesthetic appreciation of art, since the latter must in some way, to be vital, retrace the course of the creative process. But development of this point in its bearing upon aesthetic judgment and theory is another story.[3]

This brings the discussion to the problem of meaning. What then is meaning? Is meaning merely a subjective response to some objective situation. Are values really just preferences? Dewey maintains that meaning is experienced through the difference that our experience makes. One finds the meaning of love by experiencing its many dimensions (from infatuation to commitment and all the stops in between). Interpretation is therefore an essential element in the process of growth. Unless one can move from level to level of meaning within experience, no real possibility of expansion in width and depth of value is really possible. To grow as a human being demands the capacity to range through levels of depth of meaning within one's experience. This is the essence of human culture.

What is required for such cultural growth is the attainment of a delicate balance between the stable and the precarious. In nature all live beings seek this state of homeostasis. The cultural equivalent of this drive for equilibrium is experienced as the achievement of harmony. Cultural harmony balances novelty and regularity. Now this is no easy task for the two qualities appear diametrically opposed. But we must remember Dewey's refusal to accept separations. What heals the gaps between the permanent and the changing is experience itself. For what happens in an experience is a transformation of the situation into one that flows into an entirely new dimension of reality—an environmental field no longer infected by the divisions that shrink growth.

This shows that experience is not only interpretive but also cor-rective. It changes our perspective on things. It tells us that the situa-tion was not what we thought it was. We sense an imbalance in our situation. Things are not what they used to be. What was once in phase is now out of phase. What most often happens in a genuine experience is that our initial anticipations of what the situation was all about need to be corrected. "We fell in love but it didn't work out." This familiar refrain is often misinterpreted as "things happened" and love ended. What is closer to the truth is that our anticipations of what love would be like changed during the course of the relationship. Thus two paths present themselves. I can say, "It just didn't work out" and leave it at that. Or I can say, "Maybe my idea of what love is has to change." One dismisses the possibility of misinterpretation; the other builds on it. Depending on one's answer, experience stalls or grows.

This presence of an end in view right at the start points toward a crucial dimension of experience. Experience has its own pace and tempo. It follows a unique temporal pattern that emphasizes a rhythm of cumulative growth interspersed with resistances, pauses, returns, reenactments, and novel opportunities for risk taking. Experience is organic and the opposite of the mechanical. Where the mechanical repeats itself without difference, endlessly and in a serial formula, the organic is full of surprises, changes in pace, and novel expressions that take advantage of opportunities felt during the creative process. The organic includes the different within its process of formation; the mechanical merely uses it. The mechanical consists of parts arranged in external relations; the organic is created by means of its internal relations. The mechanical is preprogrammed for success and when that is thwarted, its uselessness becomes apparent. The organic finds a way around resistances. It continually reinvents itself by reason of enlarg-ing the scope of differences that it can embrace.

The tempo of the organic is rhythmic. A rhythm is a repetition with a difference. There is a sameness to the beat of its growth, but that unvarying quality is changed by novel expressions coming from the heart of its experience. Consider "The Last Rose of Summer." We study it as it presents itself to us. There are rings of growth inscaped into its form. There are unfoldings of vital expression within each petal as it curls itself around its neighbor. The bush has grown throughout the summer and now as that season fades together with its special rhythms and tempos, the last rose sums up in its beauty and goodness the varying times of this season of growth. The experience of "The Last Rose" is that of a consummation of experience wherein all the turns and twists of time are embodied in a single living creature. Through convolutions and involutions, "The Last Rose" expresses in its own unique form the rhythms of experience that made it what it is and the summer what it was. Organic time literally beats its way into the doings and undergoings that characterize the transformative, corrective, and interpretative quality of experience. To know is to appreciate.

Experience is always cadenced. It is no mere mechanical repetition of what has been going on in a particular environmental field. Experience establishes its rhythmic tempo by reason of the establishment of polarities that balance each other. For example, what unites body and mind is experience itself. Any attempt to remain satisfied with separations, divisions, and dualisms is for Dewey a surrender to the vicious gods of abstraction. The basic polarity in every experience is that of a field and its focus. A tension is established between these two elements. The rhythm that results marks out the boundaries of the struggle for balance and equilibrium. Each experience therefore has its own unique quality. The first step in analyzing any experience is to identify what is at play within the experience in question.

The cadences that are the unique signature of each experience are the expressions of the dynamic form that guides it to completion. Form harnesses the energies at play in a situation and turns them to advantage. The pressures, resistances, disappointments, successes, and accomplishments that are undergone and achieved in the course of an experience—all these elements and much more go into the final result. And even then, the scene merely shifts to another dimension of the search for balance. There is no such thing as absolute unmoving perfection in a world characterized by process:

> Experience, in other words, is a matter of *simultaneous* doings and sufferings. Our undergoings are experiments in varying the course of events; our active tryings are trials and tests of ourselves. This duplicity of experience shows itself in our happiness and misery, our successes and failures. Triumphs are dangerous when dwelt upon or lived off from; successes use themselves up. Any achieved equilibrium of adjustment with the environment is precarious because we cannot evenly keep pace with changes in the environment. They are so opposed in direction that we must choose. We must take the risk of casting our lot with one movement or the other. Nothing can eliminate all risk, all adventure; the one

thing doomed to failure is to try to keep even with the whole environment at once—that is to say, to maintain the happy moment when all
things go our way.[4]

What carries the experience forward to its conclusion is the continual reinvention of forms suitable to the experience being had. Thus
the doings and undergoings that mark experience never predict its
eventual outcome. I doubt Leonardo knew what the *Mona Lisa* looked
like before he painted it. If he did, then it was a mechanical effort lacking the inventiveness and ingenuity of a genuine organic experience.
One neither can nor should know in advance what will happen in a
significant experience.

Experience builds upon itself. It uses its past (however shallow or
deep) to advance into the future (however unknown or predictable)
and it uses the future to reflect on what is happening within the present experiential moment. The present is the moment when the measured rhythms of experience find themselves in polar opposition. For
Dewey this is the "great opportunity," for we either "grow or go." At
the moment when all doors seem closed, there may appear to the sensitive person an opportunity to do something different. This suggestion
could come from the environment itself, the person's history, or one's
goal in the future. In any case what must be understood is the fact that
all this occurs *within* experience itself. The phases of experience mark
out the moments of resistances overcome, new forms invented, old
forms reinterpreted, anticipations corrected, and goals redirected.

Experience is therefore cumulative. It advances not in a monot-
onous serial manner. It starts and stops. It hesitates. It leaps forward. It
rests. It slowly advances. It quickly pulls back. Experience does not
dwell in the past. That is nostalgia. Neither does it forecast certain
results. That is the quest for certainty, a false hope that diminishes the
human spirit and deprives us of the courage needed to persevere in the
face of difficulties. When a genuine experience is accomplished, then
the whole is seen to have been present in all the parts and each part
even in its difference is seen to be reflected in the whole. What culminates when a full experience is authentically had is the completion
of a process that began with a sense of imbalance, proceeded through
various phases, and finally reached a moment of satisfaction. The
rhythms of experience establish a balance between the push and pull
of forces alive within its environmental field. What results is a live

feeling resting on the tensions active within the experience. What was out of phase is now in phase. Whatever began the process of experience has now yielded to another way of being. And that mode itself becomes another starting point for more experience. Experience is the way in which humans (and all nature for that matter) seek stability. Each success is both a resting point as well as a starting point for the next experience. Experience breathes fire into the universe.

This is why Dewey maintains that there are two basic types of experience, that which is *instrumental* and that which is *consummatory*. Instrumental experience is the subject matter of the next chapter. Here we concentrate on the consummatory dimension. That in turn will allows us to match up this uniquely American angle of vision with some major Confucian themes.

Dewey identifies consummatory experience with deeply felt human values. His model for such felt experience is art. Understanding how a work of art "works" extends the discussion of experience in several important directions. To review: rich and full experience— what Dewey calls *consummatory*—is marked by several significant qualities. In the first place, it is made of flowing wholes that reassert themselves in varying rhythms as the experience moves forward. These wholes are transformed as the experience is undergone. In having such experiences there is a radical transformation of the field of meaning from one where imbalance and trouble ruled to one in which creative forces unite to express entirely novel ways of being in the world. This is why art is the signature mode of this way of experience. For the artist takes what is already known—material, colors, shapes, words, musical notes, melodies, cultural values and traditions—and so reconstructs them that new forms of unity and variety are provided. What began as a mere problem—how do we get in out of the rain?—turns into a Frank Lloyd Wright house.

But the introduction of novelty is not the essence of art. If that were so, any zany project would do. The work of art has several special features. A work of art lets wholes and parts work together in rhythmic tempos that increase the intensity of experience. Furthermore, it does not merely reject the past for the sake of what is new. Rather it transforms the most important aspects of the past and finds new ways to distribute those energies within the present moment. It builds the values of the past into the present. Likewise, it anticipates profoundly important aspects of the future and, thereby, makes palpable the changes culture is about to undergo. It entices us to come to grips with what is about to happen and offers important clues as to how to engage new meanings. It brings the full weight of experience to bear upon the present moment. It provides us with intense feelings. These feelings wake us to what our past has been, what our future might be like and what our present holds in its hands. All the disruptions of the past and the interruptions of the future are resolved in a consummatory moment in the present.

But that is only part of the story of a work of art. Within aesthetic experience we find a model for bringing to a satisfactory conclusion the imbalances suffered within human experience. Such an enjoyment is the result of achieving integration. The completion that marks an aesthetic experience reworks in a novel and creative fashion the resistances felt between parts and wholes within a troubled situation. What results is a consummation that is also an initiation. New adventures are made possible through new energies released by the work of art. The work of art "works" to release those dimensions of experience previously bottled up due to poor connections and a lack of purpose and direction.

A genuine consummatory experience dissolves separations and heals the splits in culture. What was previously felt as the division between form and content is now experienced as the unification of what is going on with how it is going on. The distinctions between mind and body drop away and are replaced by new feelings that convey both the resistances overcome as well as the new understandings gained. There is now a consummatory experience leading its participants into creative directions that cancel a past once filled with gaps, hesitations, and a profound lack of wholeheartedness. Energies are regathered around forms of completion that promise more insights for the future. Dammed up emotions are released. A special union of thinking and feeling now has its day. Similarly, on the social level the person and the community complement each other.

What has happened is the reconstruction of a situation previously neglected. In place of lacerations of the spirit, novel feelings of wholeness emerge—novel in the sense that they were never felt or even guessed at prior to this consummatory experience. What was once separate is now whole. A reinvigorated common sense sees relationships where once there were only isolated feelings and activities. How things fit together and why they go this way and not that way become pressing human questions. The great cultural task is to do justice to our enriched sense of the possibilities of value lurking in experience. For Dewey as for classical American philosophy in general, the mantra is always the same: "Relations, relations, relations (and then more relations)."

Consummatory experience creates modes of felt intelligence never had before. In painting, the cube becomes a factor in feeling the presence of the human body. A new arrangement of notes opens an unnoticed path to unheard sounds of joy. Domestic matters long buried are now the stuff of drama. Action becomes a form of fleshed thought as it simultaneously weds body to mind. Direction, purpose, and aim are expressed *through* the body, not merely *by* it. The body "is" full of sorrow or "is" full of tension and strain. Our eyes feel the radiance of the luminous in a particular painting. Ritual is no longer a technique. It is a part of the emerging whole that marks consummatory experiences. What are put to rest within these consummatory experiences are the dualisms so embedded in our way of viewing the world. We experience the unity in variety that is the stamp of authentic consummatory experience. It is this rhythm of the mutual adaptation of parts within an experienced whole that is the central feature of consummatory experience.

A culture that can consistently integrate its multiple dimensions so that effort is drawn onward towards ever more novel fields of experience requires certain strengths. It must provide new energies to its members so that they can create different forms of experience, even ones that challenge traditional values. Otherwise, a culture is consumed by a fatal disease: narcissism. The split between the self and the world becomes so intense that what is different must be killed if the narcissistic one is to survive. Totalitarian regimes that stifle all forms of creativity not approved in advance come into being. But the creation of the different is what great art is all about. Art helps culture press forward into unknown regions of experience.

But the truth is that sometimes consummatory experience does not happen. The issues involved are too intractable or too confused or too little understood. And then a kind of aesthetic patience must take over and experimental efforts drawn in part from previous experience and in part from risks taken by the present generation come into play. It is precisely here that culture must encourage the cultivation of the new. Consummatory experience is not mechanical. It does not deliver the goods on time, serially and without interruption. The consummatory is the organic. It deals in surprises that can only be understood by whole, free, and unfrightened human beings. When it occurs, it is a treasure for the entire society since split worlds of fact and value heal and psychic pain is reduced.

Cultures need to endorse the freedom of their members and refuse to see attacks on orthodoxy as threats to social stability. It is here that wise governments withdraw the censor and initiate campaigns of education. For a people coerced is a people incapable of summoning up the kind of commitment required to push the curve of culture forward into new uncharted territories—regions of experience and value promising deeper forms of unity needed by the community. The factor of the integer (the addition of that one thing more that catalyzes an experience mired in disruptions) only comes into play when a people is given the right to risk experimentation with cultural forms. For culture is not about enjoying pretty things or having a refined sense of beauty. That is a decadent form of culture characteristic of a society in decline. Culture is about finding forms of experience that help us stay alive, then thrive, and finally become even better at bringing together our varied worlds of experience.

Consummatory experience is the apex of vitality. It is the primary way in which human beings have historically been coaxed into successful dealings with the separations that weaken their experience. The consummatory heals the lacerations inflicted on the human soul by a culture maimed by its own abstractions. In place of isolated objects and ideas, consummatory experience initiates and then sustains a rhythm of integration just right for the cultural spirit of an age. This vibratory pulse is transmitted through various physiological, psychological, and social forms until the experience of unity is had by the community. Art is a consummation, a celebration, and a new starting point. It dissolves the resistances that previously split experience. It then proceeds to celebrate what has been achieved. In bringing about such a closure, the consummatory experience then provides a new starting point for further cultural growth.

A consummatory experience transcribes the energies at play within a culture so that acts of blending and fusion replace what was once isolated and separated. The background pervades the foreground and the foreground uses the grace of such a background of importance to heighten, detail, and finally fully express its own qualities. When this occurs, the community is helped to cooperate intelligently. It struggles to find resolutions of past difficulties and fresh insights with which to face the future. John Dewey's own words aptly summarize what goes on in this kind of experience:

> Esthetic recurrence in short is vital, physiological, functional. Relation-ships rather than elements recur, and they recur in differing contexts and with different consequences so that each recurrence is novel as well as a reminder. In satisfying an aroused expectancy, it also institutes a new longing, incites a fresh curiosity, establishes a changed suspense. The completeness of the integration of these two offices, opposed as they are in abstract conception, by the *same* means instead of by using one device to arouse energy and another to bring it to rest, measures artistry of production and perception. A well-conducted scientific inquiry discovers as it tests, and proves what it explores; it does so in virtue of a method which combines both functions. And conversation, drama, novel, and architectural construction, if there is an ordered experience, reach a stage that at once records and sums up the value of what precedes, and evokes and prophesies what is to come. Every clo-sure is an awakening, and every awakening settles something. This state of affairs defines organization of energies.[5]

Dewey and Confucius agree that human beings are primarily social. Their identity, their achievements, and their possibilities are the outcome of how they were raised. This act of "raising a child" is not simply the responsibility of parents. Rather Dewey and Confucius would argue that the act of raising a child begins with parents, extends to the immediate family and then reaches out to include the culture within which that human being lives. The failure of one citizen is an indictment of the whole culture.

As a public intellectual Dewey came to see the importance of providing an integrated cultural vision for the citizens of his time. He did this largely by trying to recapture for philosophy its traditional role as the critic of values. He did not see himself as doing something new when he spoke out on education or economics or art or science and technology. Nor was he the victim of some sort of megalomania that seduced him into thinking that he could speak about anything at any time. Dewey saw philosophy as the critic of culture and what he meant by that phrase goes straight to the heart of his philosophical vision.[6]

Remember what turned Dewey toward philosophy in the first place. It was his abiding suspicion of dualisms. Every science or humanity or art operates from a select point of view. Physicists concern themselves with atomic particles and painters concern themselves with shapes, colors, and lines. Each has a distinct perspective that allows it to pursue its own special form of excellence. This is a cultural commonplace. But for Dewey it also presents a major cultural problem. Is there no discipline that ties them together so that we can live as integrated human beings? At some level we do live well or poorly as unified human beings. How does the "live creature" live in a fractured cultural environment?[7]

Philosophy for Dewey is the effort to attain a unified vision of the values and activities dominant in our culture and to assess their worth. I have elsewhere called it normative thinking.[8] Every other mode of estimating values—art, religion, ethics, and science—establishes a particular horizon that brings along in its train a limited set of structures. What each of these shares is an organization of the real into a foreground and a background. What makes philosophy different from these other cultural pursuits is the fact that it concentrates on the adequacy of these structural modes of shaping and having an experience. Each cultural pursuit is in itself a criticism of a level and a region of experience. It asks, why paint with this technique rather than that? Or why must ideals always remain locked into a transcendental horizon that is immutable? Philosophy on the other hand asks about the most general types of horizons. Are they adequate to experience itself? What about the concept of a foreground/background structure to all events in the natural world? Is it a worthy explanation of how reality functions?

Philosophy in its role as critic has a special cultural office. It must stand up for the ultimate unification of experience even as it provides room for the particularity of its parts and the power of the relations that hold those parts together. Philosophy is that mode of reflective experience that watches over the organic unity that characterizes each authentic event of experience. Philosophy must therefore be rooted in time as a depository of past achievements. It must also look to the future as the locus of future values. And it must live in the present where the quality now affecting reality is being forged. Without philosophy as his home discipline, Dewey never could have seen widely enough or felt deeply enough to come to grips with the separations weakening the human spirit.

The other cultural pursuits proceed by way of selective abstractions that present the world from different angles and perspectives. Philosophy, on the other hand, seeks the most general cultural perspective. It challenges our most basic concepts of what is real. It asks whether our relations with each other are just and satisfactory. It seeks to provide an adequate response to the question of the ultimate meaning of life. It asks if those in authority are carrying out their responsibilities in a worthy manner. It tries to ascertain the meaning of the most important concepts in our cultural world. It seeks *wisdom*.

Now what is wisdom? It is certainly connected with knowledge but it is not the same as the possession of elegant theories and indisputable facts. It is concerned with values, but it does not proclaim dogmatic views as to the nature of the good. It is not silent about wrongdoings and evil but it is not simply a moral scold. It is grounded in and has to be won through long experience. It is not the work of amateurs and at the same time, it is not the result of any special expertise. Its possession by a sage is marked by both action and contemplation. It is directly connected with the world of everyday affairs but it can move beyond such perspectives to a wider view of what is really happening.

Philosophy, as its name implies, is the love of wisdom. It is not the possession of wisdom itself but rather the effort to become intimate with wisdom. It is a discipline grounded in fallibilism. It can learn from its mistakes, and its history is therefore organically connected to its proper development. Even the most contrary theories are part of its heritage, for to know what is wrong is also to know what to avoid and why. Philosophy must also display a disciplined character. It is not merely the sharing of opinions on a talk show. It has to know how to apply its insights and when to hold back. Philosophy is therefore the crowning achievement of an experience-based culture. Without it we cannot go very far in our pursuit of the good. With it we can at least know the nature of our errors as well as which path is more likely to bring wisdom.

At the same time philosophy is always in danger of becoming deracinated and abstract. It easily loses sight of its goal of wisdom and can settle for the empty enjoyment of elegant theories. As a result, it is continually exposed to the danger of being separated from experience. This is why it must always be tested in real life. It has to be adequate to our experience and match up to what we actually feel in the situations of which philosophy so eloquently speaks. Philosophy is therefore poetic in the sense that it tries feebly to express the feelings that actually go into particular experiences. Philosophy seeks also to make thinking a practical instrument that can be effective in the real world. And finally, philosophy is about identifying and creating the most successful ways of communicating the meanings of the feelings and ideas fashioned in the course of our cultural growth and development.

Our reality is one in which relationships are more important than objects and things. It is how we connect with our world that determines its value for us. At the same time this is not an invitation to a rampant subjectivism, for the world also has its relations and conditions that we must learn to respect and understand. Therefore experience is, as said before, both a doing and an undergoing. Philosophy studies these relations in their widest contexts and seeks to determine their character. They show themselves to us in the feelings experienced through the orders of the world. Physical compulsion and emotional discharge are not the same but neither are they so widely different. Similarly, the establishment of effective habits of character mirrors the general traits of order experienced in the natural world. Once again, they are different but what also makes them generically the same is a chief concern of philosophy. All this is congruent with Dewey's primary complaint about his culture: *No more separations!*

Thus philosophy takes seriously the radical situatedness of the relations that make up experience. There can be *no fixed ends* in nature or culture. Furthermore, there is no ultimate good that beckons us either in this life or some other. What is really here and what is really our destiny is the process of discovering new and more satisfying connections with both the natural and human environment. Therefore wisdom is a kind of practical intelligence that is directed toward more and more consummatory experience through more and more effective instrumental experience. This is what allows philosophy to unite the abstract and the concrete. For philosophy is the critic of abstractions insofar as these inevitably partial perspectives do or do not do justice to concrete experience.

Philosophy is a direct attempt to live life fully in the face of the radical contingency infecting our experience. We really do not know what is going to happen. This fact of life must be engaged. Philosophy's obligation is to lay down the most effective framework for confronting the task of living creatively in a universe of chance. This is why experimentalism is so important for cultural growth. Without a disciplined way to approach the contingencies of life, human beings are the consistent victims of the inconsistencies characteristic of a process universe. To learn is to experience uncertainty and make something good out of it. Thus learning is as much about how our heart feels as it is about how our mind thinks. To learn is to establish effective habits of felt intelligence that can be concretely embodied in practical human activity. The truth of such attempts to widen and deepen experience is to be found in the differences that such effort makes in our lives. These consequences are the carryover of value from the past into the future by way of the present. The instrumental leads to the consummatory, which in turn releases new energies useful for further growth.

Philosophy therefore seeks to establish the most concrete contact with reality by formulating the widest and deepest possible view of what it means to experience the world in which we dwell. Given the vastness of the task, it is inevitable that failure and error block philosophy's progress. Nevertheless, there is a master key: *experience*. Philosophy's cultural duty will continue to be misunderstood as long as it is confused with the other cultural pursuits. The best way to avoid this error is to make clear the kind of knowing involved in philosophy's use of experience. Art uses material to express consummatory moments of unity and difference. Religion grapples with the sense of transcendence and immanence that haunts our worldly experience. Ethics and science concentrate on the instrumental dimension of experience. Technology applies the results of scientific instrumental experience. But when philosophy encounters experience and seeks to express its generic features and basic traits, it finds that the vocabulary and theoretical framework of the particular pursuits (art, religion, ethics, science, and technology) are not up to the task. Their abstractions are too selective and each in its own way leaves out something central to experience.

Experience, philosophically understood, is wider than the act of merely knowing objects. Dewey therefore assigns philosophy a double task. Indeed, it must continue to strive to understand the goals and means of particular cultural pursuits. But it must also find out what it is that brings all such cultural pursuits together. For even as each takes a uniquely individual approach to experience, each at the same time is grounded in experience itself. There must therefore be some common ground out of which these different versions of experience arise. What is it? How is it encountered? These are the primary philosophical questions. Philosophy's answer, according to Dewey, ought to be that the most general and concrete dimension of experience is the felt presence of value. Everything that constitutes experience is at its heart saturated in a particular quality. The very fact that it exists announces that something worthwhile has actually happened. We live in a world charged with importances of different kinds.

Now there ought to be a cultural discipline dedicated to the discovery and articulation of these forms of value. It must seize the cardinal dimensions of these events. It must show how they develop and out of what soil they grow. It must also respond to the question, what is their destiny? Furthermore, how they link up to other experiences and what emerges from these relations is also part of philosophy's vocation. Now all these questions are deliberately put in the widest and therefore potentially most abstract manner. For philosophy must seek wisdom about such matters and wisdom is only wisdom when it can be effective in the widest possible manner.

Philosophy is the search for the most sweeping traits of existence. What it finds first of all is that existence comes about within situations. Then it understands that these situations are marked by a character that Dewey calls experience. This experiential dimension concerns the emergence of actual values that play out their destiny within the scope afforded them by other experiences. Philosophy is the search for the value expressed by experiential events arising out of particular situations. It must answer the questions, why? how? and what? Its answer must be general enough to apply to experiences had at different times. But such generality must prove its effectiveness by showing how such answers can make a difference in the lives of human beings. Here is the origin of the pragmatist's concern for results and consequences. What matters most is *the difference* such experiences make. The difference made is the value expressed. If there is no difference after the experience has been had, then there was no experience to be had. When the value is absent, so too is the reality that it expresses. Put another way: what happens either makes a difference or it did not happen.

But philosophy's cultural office is not exhausted by the satisfaction of such universal (metaphysical) questions. It also must judge the value of these values. This is another reason why Dewey calls philosophy "the criticism of criticisms." It is not merely a matter of taking an inventory of cultural achievements and ascertaining what is of interest and what is not. Rather what is needed is some normative measure whereby the purpose and direction of such activities can be identified. Dewey found in Darwin's evolutionary understanding of the processes of nature a gauge by which the excellence and quality of a culture can be appreciated. He called it growth and saw it in evolutionary terms. Every experience is also a potential interference with the patterns of nature. Whether it will thrive or perish depends on just how successful it is in altering established patterns or fitting in with them. Similar judgments attend all cultural pursuits, be they aesthetic, religious, ethical, scientific, or technological.

We live in a world marked by the alternating presence of the stable and the precarious. We seek homeostasis, and when we find it, we then seek to prolong its presence. It is what we need in order to have the confidence and energy to go forth and meet new adventures. Stability in our lives is never permanent for that is not our lot. We live in a sea of changing circumstances and do not control the universe. Still, there are stopping points and when they occur, we can use them to nourish our spirit and gather ourselves. At the same time we meet the unforeseen and are thrown by it. Often we feel as though we will perish. Life at times is as precarious as it is stable. When so afflicted, our natural tendency is to run and hide (and sometimes this is all that we actually can do). But culture is supposed to ease our confrontations with the perils of existence. Therefore its quality and goodness can be judged by just how well it helps us endure and then grow out of precarious experiences.

The primary standard for culture is growth. Does it help us encounter the losses we experience and grow from them? Does it help us appreciate our gains and be nourished by them? Positive answers to both questions mean that our culture is helping us experience what is best in life—a pattern of balance whereby the bad is ameliorated and the good is encouraged to grow in its place. Nature ever advances into novelty and along with it, so does the human race. This means that how we deal with the new is the major question facing humankind.

The problem includes how we shall deal with our past, its values, and its achievements. It also involves how we presently live today and what portion of our resources is to be given over to dealing with the presence of the new in our lives. Finally, the cultural question also brings the future to bear upon both the present and the past. Thus the organic flow of time insinuates itself into our cultural being. The rhythms of life are characterized by the real presence of the stable and the precarious, the new and the old, the growing and the decaying. To a naturalist like Dewey, there should be no surprise about the fact that culture also shares these fundamental features.

As in nature, experience and culture are locked in a dance of life and death. Only here we are dealing with the values achieved by human beings and their worth in sustaining our growing presence on this earth. As a cultural enterprise philosophy seeks to provide the widest possible perspective from which to answer such questions. The wisdom of its vision is to be judged by the effectiveness of the outlook it provides.

❖

Working Connections with Confucius: Dao, De, and Ren

The development of working connections between Dewey and Confucius rests upon a clear understanding of the patterned quality of Chinese thinking and language. By pattern I mean that there are always levels of relations at work in any Chinese concept or word. The three ideas we are about to explore—*dao*, *de*, and *ren*—are excellent examples of this feature. A similar quality of coherence is also at the heart of Dewey's thoughts on culture and experience. Just as Dewey's concept of experience demanded a necessary reference to other ideas, so also Chinese thought demands a similar "correlation."[9]

What is needed to begin the process of effective communicating on a global level are connections that work to bring cultures together. This coming together is not about creating simple-minded agreements. It is much more a matter of mutual understanding. Nothing therefore could be more important at the beginning of such a process than a clear understanding of how different cultures understand the fundamental forms and structures of reality. Dewey's notion of experience has provided us an American perspective. Is there a Confucian idea that connects with Dewey's concept of experience?

There are three interlocking ideas that shape the Confucian worldview: *dao*, *de* and *ren*. An understanding of each concept and its relations to the others will provide a basis for the rest of this study. Confucius is always concerned with finding the right way to handle a situation. "Way" is the conventional translation of the Chinese word *dao*. Exploring its depth of meaning is fundamental to grasping a real understanding of the Confucian sense of reality. I claim that it is the Confucian equivalent of Dewey's primary concept of experience. To find the way is to get one's bearings in a realm of constantly changing situations. Walking on such a path ought to bring one into the most productive course of action.

I also believe that Dewey's idea of growth is the closest analog we can get for understanding the experience of walking an appropriate *dao*. Like growth, finding the *dao* is always a personal matter. For it is not the *dao* that shapes human behavior as much as it is the human who enlarges the *dao* by reason of experience. Thus, "The Master said it is the person who is able to broaden the way (*dao*), not the way that broadens the person" (*Analects* 15.29)[10] Recall Dewey's understanding of growth as a way of acting that establishes the deepest and widest associations within a particular situation or event. The way is to be personalized by the experiencer; otherwise, it becomes mechanical, rote, and sterile. Like experience, the way must evoke intense feelings that will fuel the effort needed to go the distance. It must summon up liveliness. Equally so is the way's quality of being engaged with the matter at hand. The problems encountered on the way must be met with honesty and transparency. Hypocrisy is direct evidence of having lost the way.

> The Master said: "From fifteen, my heart-and-mind was set upon learning; from thirty I took my stance; from forty I was no longer doubtful; from fifty I realized the propensities of heaven; from sixty my ear was attuned; from seventy I could give my heart-and-mind free rein without overstepping the boundaries.[11]

The reference to hearing the tune confirms the fact that like Dewey, the way is always aesthetic in the sense that our educated and trained feelings will give us a sense of direction as we proceed down the road. Things feel right or they feel off. These are not mere subjective feelings but rather the result of long and arduous training and discipline. When form and feeling begin to fall together in a habitual way, then intense, engaged experience comes about. Every athlete, musician, artist, and teacher knows this to be true. When one hits the mark, a path to development that is continuous and moving toward wholeness opens up. When an appropriate *dao* is experienced, then imbalances, instabilities, and overwrought or understressed dimensions of reality receive new direction from the corrective interpretations embodied in every fit way of being human. These qualities of intense engaged feelings receive their ultimate justification when the community within which they take place recognizes their excellence. What *dao* does so effectively is unite thought and action, morality and stubborn fact, body and mind, individual and community. *Dao* succeeds in overcoming the dualisms that haunted Dewey's vision of nineteenth- and twentieth-century culture.

As Confucius puts in the *Analects*:

> The Master said: "Make an earnest commitment to the love of learning and be steadfast to the death in service to the efficacious way. Do not enter a state in crisis, and do not tarry in one that is in revolt. Be known when the way prevails in the world, but remain hidden when it does not. It is a disgrace to remain poor and without rank when the way prevails in a state; it is a disgrace to be wealthy and of noble rank when it does not.[12]

Dao represents an experiential path that is taken. When it is so taken then beneficial order can grow. Everything depends on the reception of the way by the culture within which it is experienced. To betray the way is never good but to protect it when it is not appreciated is an act of courage and wisdom. In this way the *dao* is normative, for it sets out the standards for behavior in all circumstances. And this is so even in circumstances where no one respects it. Nothing could be better proof that the *dao* is a process and not a result, object, or thing. As a process, *dao* calls for deftness, subtlety, and awareness of one's situation. As the Master says on one occasion, "It is not that I aspire to be an eloquent talker, but rather that I hate inflexibility."[13]

And at the heart of *dao* is the sensibility that takes in the community as the ultimate measure by which to judge one's actions. Whether it is for the sake of growth, social justice, peace, or insight into finding the way through difficulties, one characteristic of *dao* stands out for Confucius:

> The Master said: "Zeng, my friend! My way is bound together with one continuous strand."
> Master Zeng replied, "Indeed."
> When the Master had left, the disciples asked, "What was he referring to?"
> Master Zeng said, "The way of the Master is doing one's utmost and putting oneself in the other's place, nothing more.[14]

As a way of being *dao* aims at excellence. This brings us to the second Confucian theme, *de*. Since forging a *dao* is an intensely personal experience, way seekers have adopted a certain style or mode of being. This is what accounts for the expressive character that accompanies their actions. As a style of being, walking on a *dao* is revealed by certain clues. Just as we can detect a friend walking in the distance by her gait, carriage, and other habitual traits, so also there is a style of action that is characteristic of one who walks on a *dao*. That quality is the achievement of *de*, the excellent. This excellence has several shared characteristics no matter the personal idiosyncrasies of the way walker. First, it is in harmony with its biological and cultural environments. Second, this excellence is such that it succeeds in gaining the best that can be achieved in a given set of circumstances. I cannot expect a kindergarten student to master the intricacies of algebraic thinking. There is a correlation between what the situation can handle and the kind of power of transformation that *de* can bring to it. But whatever the outcome, *de* can always be understood as having achieved the truth residing in the situation. This is because Chinese thinking sees truth as the carryover of past values into the present moment and relevant future. *De* seeks the normative excellence possible in the given situation. The last characteristic of the way walker who exhibits *de* in carriage and action is that the community recognizes that something better and different is now available for experience.

De is to be understood as an attractive good. It draws others to its side and makes the way appealing. Its power to bring others farther on the way and farther toward excellence is caught in this Confucian analogy:

The Master said: "Governing with excellence (*de*) can be compared to being the North Star: the North Star dwells in place, and the multitude of stars pay it tribute.[15]

The word "better" is the term Dewey uses to summarize his ethical theory. It is the duty of humans to ameliorate situations. And this excellence is brought about by experiencing deeper, wider, and more intense connections within the associated life of the persons involved. To be environmentally relevant is to be a constructive force within the biological and cultural values that make up one's region of experience. *De* names this achievement. What should be experienced when such excellence is had is an intense feeling of growth.

What needs stressing in this explanation of *de* is its communal aspect. Like Dewey, Confucius had little trust in the theory of the "great man" or the single individual who all alone conquers evil and restores the good. What prevented a correct understanding of much of Dewey's thought was the ingrained American *ideal of the individual*. This mythical being has never existed and never will. And yet in our culture and in our self-image it retains great force. It is the gunslinger, the hero, the lonely creator, the one person who can save us all. Be it Clint Eastwood, Ronald Reagan, or the Pope, that one individual cannot do all alone what is portrayed as being pulled off. This myth of the individual quickly transforms itself into another delusional state, the myth of the necessity of hierarchy. All power, grace, and strength should flow downward from the great to the small. When these two delusions are welded together we get the kind of arrogant ignorance that ruins environments, neglects the poor, and tramples on the weak. Standing against this fallacy of the Solitary Great One is the ideal of ecological *de*, or excellence. From this point of view every member of a community contributes to the web of relations that makes up the order that benefits all. Just as no single member deserves all the credit, so also no single member or group deserves all the rewards. Value is spread out ecologically. Excellent growth is enjoyed throughout the environment.[16] What determines the *de* of a situation is what is needed within that situation. No one has special preeminence or a pre-ordained right to determine what is necessary.

De begins as individual in the sense that anyone walking a *dao* must forge one's own path. But if this chosen *dao* is going to be successful, it must sooner or later turn toward the reality of its own envi-

ronment and find there the tools necessary to rectify mistakes, overcome imbalances, and restore excellence to the connections that bind
humans together. Novelty, creative individuality, the insights of the
genius, the uniqueness of different perspectives—all these special
values must ultimately prove their merit by improving the life of the
many. Confucius expresses directly this social obligation:

> The Master said: "Lead the people with administrative injunctions and
> keep them orderly with penal law, and they will avoid punishment but
> will be without a sense of shame. Lead them with excellence (de) and
> keep them orderly through ritual propriety (li) and they will develop a
> sense of shame, and moreover, will order themselves.[17]

Shame here has the sense that one has harmed another and therefore
has also harmed oneself. It is the appropriate human response to vio-
lating the most precious of human bonds, those that tie us to one
another. For Confucius the way to helping others lies in accumulating
excellence so as to be of service to another:

> Zizhang inquired about accumulating excellence (de) and sorting things
> out when in a quandary. The Master replied, "To take doing one's
> utmost, making good on one's word, and seeking out what is appropri-
> ate as one's main concerns, is to accumulate excellence. To simultane-
> ously love and hate someone, and thus to simultaneously want this
> person to live and die, is to be in a quandary. 'You surely do not gain for-
> tune this way; you only get something different.'"[18]

In these words one finds the roots of a social ethics grounded in each
individual's pursuit of excellence. Nothing is a solitary affair, for all is
connected to the community, even one's deepest and most private
emotions. The importance of de in terms of the Confucian worldview
is made clear by the fact that there can be an excess of excellence:
Zixia said, "In matters which demand surpassing excellence, one never
oversteps the mark; in minor affairs one has some latitude."[19] And to
conclude these remarks on de with the Master's own words:

> The Master said: "To fail to cultivate excellence (de), to fail to practice
> what I learn, on coming to understand what is appropriate in the cir-
> cumstances to fail to attend to it, and to be unable to reform conduct
> that is not productive—these things I worry over.[20]

All this brings us to the most innovative contribution Confucius has made to human culture: the idea of *ren*. Simply stated, it says that to be a human being is an accomplishment, not a title given one at birth. It says further that it is the responsibility of one's familial, social, and cultural institutions to assist in the processes whereby an individual becomes *ren*. No term is more crucial for understanding the underlying consonance between Dewey and Confucius than this concept of *ren*. *Ren* has traditionally been translated as "humanity" or "benevolence." The terms are not rich enough to capture the feel of the Confucian idea. "Humanity" is too general a term and its blandness leaves us wondering what is so unique about the Confucian idea of being human. "Benevolence" is a better term for it points towards two important characteristics of *ren*. Benevolence suggests that the condition of other human beings is vitally important for our own humanity. It also implies that our own health depends upon the health and happiness of others. We are, as has been said before, incurably social beings. To live humanly is to live together.

Ames and Rosemont in their benchmark translation of the *Analects* translate *ren* with a set of phrases: "authoritative conduct, to act authoritatively, and authoritative person."[21] These translations convey a number of levels of meaning. They imply that a human being must undergo a process of growth. The sense of "authoritative" therefore means to grow or create oneself through appropriate behavior within one's culture. *Ren* is therefore thoroughly consonant with Dewey's primary normative measure, growth. Once again, growth for Dewey means the laying down of deeper, richer working connections with others. Just as an author crafts the pattern of meanings that make up a character, so also human beings author themselves into existence by reason of the choices made within different situations. These choices are not mere intellectual exercises. Rather they are experiential *daos* that move one towards or away from the excellence available within particular concrete circumstances. Conditions may hamper or reduce what is possible but our *ren* ought to move us towards what is best for all concerned rather than simply what is important to ourselves. Social well-being depends entirely on the effective presence of *ren*:

> The Master said: "In taking up one's residence, it is the presence of authoritative persons (*ren*) that is the greatest attraction. How can anyone be called wise who, in having the choice, does not seek to dwell among authoritative people?"[22]

Without a community of authoritative persons, education, cultural forms, communal judgments, and the exercise of authority would come to a halt. Excellence and the pursuit of the best would be stymied and the energies needed to bring forth the *de* potentially residing in everyday situations would be sapped. Mediocrity and worse threatens the community.

Similarly, the perseverance needed to found and sustain traditions of excellence would be lacking. For it is only through longtime practice in the service of the good that strong social foundations can be set down. A similar sensibility infuses Confucius's understanding of the *dao* of *de*:

> The Master said, "Those persons who are not authoritative (*ren*) are neither able to endure hardship for long, nor to enjoy happy circumstances for any period of time. Authoritative persons are content in being authoritative; wise persons flourish in it."[23]

The difference between *ren* and the concept of the individual is jarring for the Western person. Once the importance of the social environment is understood as the very source of our human being, then all our institutions become cherished tools by which we can grow into human beings. Education is not just training for a job. It is a *dao* conducting us into the richness of associated life. Employment is not just a means to earn a living. It is vital that it also be charged with meaning and dignity. The family structure is the starting point for this growth into social being and every other social institution must also be seen as a *dao* for growing into our humanity. The purpose of life is not to secure my own individual happiness in as free a way as possible:

> The Master said: "I have yet to meet people who are truly fond of authoritative conduct (*ren*) and who truly abhor behavior contrary to it. There are none superior to those who are fond of authoritative conduct. And those who abhor behavior contrary to it, in becoming authoritative themselves, will not allow such conduct to attach itself to them. Are there people who, for the space of a single day, have given their full strength to authoritative conduct? I have yet to meet them. As for lacking the strength to do so, I doubt there are such people—at least I have yet to meet them."[24]

The opposite of such an attitude has prompted others to speak of the American version of the free market as "cowboy capitalism."

When one takes a cold, hard look at the level of crime, violence, drug addiction, and family decay now present in American society, the cost of our material well-being must be questioned.

In the end it is the quality of our experience that determines our humanity. Dewey and Confucius agree on this and the Chinese were quite right to call him a "Second Confucius." The working connections between American and Chinese culture begin with a shared vision of the general traits of existence. Our experience tells us that life is precarious, that stability requires hard work, that this work cannot be done alone, and that what we undergo and suffer should be measured by the depth and variety of our relations with others. The interconnections between *dao*, *de*, and *ren* establish an effective framework within which other working connections between Confucius and Dewey can be identified. Without a generous focus (*de*), contemporary theoretical thinking will lack width, breadth, and depth. Its shallowness will reveal itself as soon as the hard work of global dialogue takes place. An adequate cultural perspective devoid of suspicion and hidden assumptions is necessary if a tradition of civility is to be created and maintained. *Dao* is to be understood as making a way for such a global achievement. The social excellence associated with the concept of *ren* results from an attitude of open understanding. It brings about behavior rooted in an attitude of deference.

Before moving to those dimensions of this study, it is good to remember these words of the Master:

> If anyone could be said to have effected proper order while remaining nonassertive, surely it was Shun. What did he do? He simply assumed an air of deference and faced due south.[25]

2

Felt Intelligence

Overcoming Dualisms

Of all the separations wounding contemporary culture none is more lethal than the split between the body and mind. It has become a permanent fixture of our intellectual landscape. The publication of Descartes's *Meditations* (1650) marks its formal introduction into philosophical history, but Western thinkers have long harbored great suspicions about the body's place in the search for wisdom. The major reason for this has been twofold. First, there is the general untrustworthiness of our sense knowledge. The stick that appears bent in the water is the classic instance used against the body as a source of knowing. But far more important, at least for our time, has been the fact the body is the source of our emotional life. We *feel* the world with and through our bodies. And feelings are notoriously difficult for philosophers to handle. They shift and change. They carry great weight in our decisions. Their sources are hidden from us. Different people have different feelings about the same issues. They can sweep us away and they can paralyze us. They are extremely unruly aspects of our human character.

And yet what would life be like without feelings? A sterile way of life would replace the liveliness of our existence. Information—dried, fast frozen, and ready to use—would become the instrument by which persons and communities judge their world. What would be lost is the felt sense of value that grounds our way of being in the world. Meaning would fade away and be replaced by data. The responsibility to carry out human judgment, always fraught with difficulty and the possibility of error, would be traded in for the security of statistical analysis. Numbers would be substituted for argument and reason. Machines would make irrefutable decisions. Human beings would become resources to be quantified. Life would flatten out and intensity, depth, and width of experience would be lost.

Dewey's philosophy has a deep reverence for science. He saw it as the spirit of our age and considered it a boon to humankind. But he was also aware of its dangers. One way of reading his philosophy is to see it as a lifelong effort to put heart back into a deracinated scientific method. His way of infusing life into the abstractions of the scientific method was to emphasize the aesthetic dimension of experience as the foundation of genuine human knowing. This fusion of the scientific and the aesthetic constitutes Dewey's most important contribution to a global philosophy. It fills the breach between body and mind. It brings together thought and feeling. It welds fact and value together. It heals the split between feeling and thinking.

I call such a human act *felt intelligence*.[1] It marks an advance on a naive reliance on science as the ultimate source of human knowing. It brings the human body into full play and puts it at the disposal of human culture as a source of wisdom and intelligence. It makes possible the unification of ethics and aesthetics. It saves science from self-destructing into a cult that worships abstraction. It also takes away the priesthood of the expert and forces science to make sense to common people. Felt intelligence is what Dewey means by the need to establish continuity between means and ends. It is therefore similar to the attitude of the artist when at work:

> Long brooding over conditions, intimate contact associated with keen interest, thorough absorption in a multiplicity of allied experiences, tend to bring about judgments which we then call "intuitive"; but they are true judgments, because they are based on intelligent selection and estimation, with solution of a problem as the controlling standard. Possession of this capacity makes the difference between the artist and the bungler.[2]

This chapter examines the felt background of what Dewey calls "instrumental" experience. It introduces the important theme of inquiry and argues for a "working connection" between what Dewey means by *inquiry* and what Confucius means by *li*. Through this comparative analysis a way of repairing the disastrous disconnect between our bodies and minds and our thoughts and feelings opens up. *Daos* of healing suggest themselves.

Instrumental experience is fundamental to all forms of natural existence, for it marks the advent of intelligence at work in the world. The beaver dams his pond and the human being resolves an architectural problem involving the carrying weight of outside walls. Dewey is often thought of as offering a crass materialistic view of the human being as merely a problem solver. Nothing could be farther from the truth. For Dewey every difficulty overcome is a sign of intelligence in action. The resistances undergone are the problems worked through in the course of experience. Experience is an affair of participation, not a spectator sport. Instrumental experience is not confined to an unending series of problems to be fixed. Remember: *There are no separations.* We are part of the problem and we are transformed while working through it. This is because the instrumental dimension of experience is the sign of the presence of intelligence at work. We learn who we are when we engage resistances and resolve issues. The reactions we develop when faced with failure, disruptions, disappointments—in a word, *problems*—lay out further fields of experience that either move us forward into deeper connections with the world or block the road to further growth. We all know people that never quite "get it." They also never grow.

Instrumental experience opens up a space within which fundamental change can take place. It provides a place where the light of intelligence can illuminate dark corners and confused situations. To be a part of these experiences is also to be part of the changes had when the experience is over. Here again, it is often not so much success that matters as it is what we learn when actually confronting resistances. In fact, so important is instrumental experience for Dewey that he gives it a special name, *inquiry*, by which he means the ways in which human beings move from troubled and problematic situations to ones that are more settled and less precarious:

> *Inquiry is the controlled or directed transformation of an indeterminate situation into one that is so determinate in its constituent distinctions and relations as to convert the elements of the original situation into a unified whole.*[3]

Now this decidedly abstract definition requires further discussion in order to bring out its full import. In the first place inquiry requires that we understand the connections of this particular situation with the past. Nothing occurs in isolation and the bonds uniting us with the past are as important as the ones to be discovered in the future. Time is organic and within it will be found the keys to understanding the troubles irritating the present moment—once again, no more separations. Second, inquiry also must define the problem as carefully as it can (this is the meaning of the word "determinate"). In fact, seeing all the dimensions of the problem often resolves the problem itself. Having the intelligence to ask, "What is really going on here?" is the first step toward finding a solution. One moves from the fuzziness of the indeterminate to the clarity of the determinate. Third, one must determine the problem exactly as it asserts itself in this particular situation. To have that flash of intuition whereby we grasp what is going on and how it binds together past problems and future opportunities is the essential moment in inquiry. This insight into the problem is achieved when we are able to create a symbol that can carry the weight and meaning of the problem in all its resistances and consequences. Thus it is not enough merely to solve this particular problem. Rather, reason must organize the facts in the case so that their experiential meaning comes to the fore in a compelling manner. This fourth element of inquiry guarantees that the intimate relation between facts and values will not be forgotten. Lastly, what occurs within a successful pattern of inquiry is the reconstruction of common sense. It is only when the community itself can say, "Now we see" that the inquiry has come to an end.

Instrumental experience is therefore always marked by the presence of cooperative intelligence. This is real intellectual work performed by real people struggling together with real problems. What Dewey has done is force us to recognize how special, how dignified, and how difficult such labor really is. Rather than passing over such work as merely another problem solved, he demands that we celebrate these achievements as the special contribution of the human soul to the growth of experience. What we do together is always more powerful than what is done alone. For just as the concept of experience is the key to no more separations, so also, as we shall see, is community the path to the deepest and most valuable experiences:

> To learn to be human is to develop through the give-and-take of communication an effective sense of being an individually distinctive

member of a community; one who understands and appreciates its beliefs, desires and methods, and who contributes to a further conversion of organic powers into human resources and values.[4]

Therefore the solutions found to problems are much more than successful means/ends experiences. Rather, the truths found within instrumental experience carry value over from one generation to another and from one difficulty—personal, social, or cultural—to another. Truth is indeed to be found in the consequences of an action, but that means the difference such truths make. The difference made is that of an opportunity for richer, more stable, more vital, and more coherent connections with the world of our peers. When instrumental experience is successful, the community experiences truth as the carry-over of value from the past to the present and toward the future. The purpose of instrumentalism is not to be found in an incessant drive toward fixing whatever has gone wrong. Nor is it merely another, more efficient way to worship what William James called "the bitch goddess, success." Truly successful instrumental experience must inevitably culminate in the other type of experience of which Dewey speaks—the *consummatory*:

> [It] is mere ignorance that leads then to the conception that connection of art and esthetic perception with experience signifies a lowering of their significance and dignity. Experience in the degree in which it *is* experience is heightened vitality. Instead of signifying being shut within one's own private feelings and sensations, it signifies active and alert commerce with the world; at its height it signifies complete interpenetration of self and the world of objects and events. Instead of signifying surrender to caprice and disorder, it affords our sole demonstration of a stability that is not stagnation but is rhythmic and developing. Because experience is the fulfillment of an organism in its struggles and achievements, it is art in germ. Even in its rudimentary forms, it contains the promise of that delightful perception which is the esthetic experience.[5]

The relation between aesthetics and ethics has always been a prominent theme in American philosophy. Dewey is universally regarded as the most important figure in American thought and culture and he is certainly the philosopher who most clearly articulates in a systematic manner the major insights and doctrines of American naturalism and pragmatism. This is especially true of his understanding of the connection between aesthetics and ethics. In following out these connections we can directly experience American philosophy's effort to unite these seemingly separated aspects of human life and culture. The goal is unity—new in form, new in activity, new in results, and new in transformed experience.

Let us go back to the beginnings of American experience as it was had by Europeans encountering for the first time a wild nature. What they needed was a clearing so that they could get their bearings. The same thing occurred each and every time they pushed the frontiers of their experience farther westward. Now this is not the place to begin a prolonged discussion of the abuses heaped on the land and the native population by such activity. Evidence for such failure is abundant and the requirement for corrective measures is self-evident. Rather, what I wish to emphasize and explore is this peculiar need itself. Why strive for an opening? Why insist on an unobstructed view? I believe it was grounded as much in an unconscious wish to get away from the strictures of a confining form of civilization as it was in a need to have open land to till. The European settler was throwing off the bonds that afflicted his experience, both economic and spiritual.[6]

Now the fundamental tool the American settler used to carry out this project was the ax. And perhaps the one he had in his hand was heavily decorated with ornamental features and refinements. Maybe it was even a ceremonial one handed down within his family from generation to generation. Now what was the settler's ultimate judgment on this ax? Was it not, Does it work? Does it do its job? Does it cut down trees? I do not think the idea of beauty as refined decoration entered his mind at all. Neither was he especially interested in the history of this ax. As we might say today, he was interested in the functional excellence of his instrument. All else was strictly secondary.

In this not so imaginary tale, I have introduced a key notion for understanding Dewey's concept of the relation between aesthetics and ethics. I have employed the term *instrumental*. As previously emphasized, it can only be fully understood when placed in a coherent relation with its apparent opposite, the *consummatory*. It is precisely this effort to overcome the separation between these two qualities that marks the heart and soul of the connection between aesthetics and ethics in American philosophy. They are to be understood as different dimensions of experience that require each other for their full expression and realization. They are different but not opposed.

Understanding why this is so requires a brief review of Dewey's metaphysics of experience.[7] For him the final real things that make up the world are not the material objects of Anglo-American empiricism. Nor are they results or aspects of mind at work as in Kantian or Hegelian forms of idealism. What is most real in the world are situations that are always in process. It is movement, change, transition, and their consequences that mark out the most important features of nature and culture. There is a principle of unrest working at the heart of reality. The upshot is that the universe is always plunging forward into novelty. The new and the different are what greet human beings every day of their lives. Just how to deal with this creative imperative is the main task of ethics. And to anticipate somewhat, ethics needs aesthetics in order to do justice to this ultimate character of what is really real.

Now for Dewey creativity does not happen all by itself. It is always situated within specific rhythms and realities. Furthermore, each of these situations has a dual character. On the one hand, it is somewhat continuous with past situations; on the other, it differs from that which was. All reality therefore swings between two poles: the familiar and the different. This means that at any given time a situation can be either in gear with its environment or wildly at variance with what is happening. Thus Dewey tells us that all human experience oscillates between the stable and the precarious. Ethics is to be understood as the effort to come to grips with this scene of alternating moods of safety and adventure.

As we have seen, Dewey names this most fundamental feature of reality *experience*, by which he means the organic interactions that occur within situations. Now every experience is some combination of the same and the different. There is continuity between what has been going on and what is going on and what will go on. But the degrees of identity and difference can vary dramatically. This is why Dewey uses the phrases "in phase" and "out of phase" to describe the basic rhythms involved in every experience. What human beings need is some degree of balance between the difference that is continually sweeping over them and the sameness that can cause an onset of sterility and boredom. It is precisely here that beauty contributes so importantly to the experience of the good life.

Experience itself reflects this alternation between difference and sameness. It consists of a series of doings and undergoings. What is done entails the action of the agent involved in the experience itself.

What is undergone are the resistances endured by that same agent as the experience proceeds to its conclusion. Now encounters with these resistances are precisely the moments when intelligence can emerge as an important factor in the process of gaining satisfactory results. Thus experience on the human level always entails the presence of an active intelligence. This is basically what Dewey means by the term *instrumental*. For an instrument is what allows the achievement of an end. A good ax is one that cuts down trees in an efficient and safe manner.

Experience is thoroughly normative since its coming to be is really the arrival of a form of value. As Dewey is at pains to assert, *something happens*. It is not *any* thing that happens. Rather *some* thing happens. There is the emergence of something unique, irreducible, fresh and novel. Now what happens is a matter of importance for it makes a difference by reason of its place in the stream of events that constitutes its field of experience. It faces a past and to some degree transforms it. It faces a future and to some degree anticipates it. It does all this within the boundaries of the present. The truth of what happens lies in the consequences that follow from its existence.

To estimate the truth of anything is not merely to record its factual presence in the world of experience. Rather, since everything that comes to be is a value, the truth of any emergent experience resides in its power to carry over the value of the past into the present and to project value into the future by reason of its efficacy in the present. To judge ethically is therefore to measure in a normatively sensitive manner the values brought about by the experience in question. This act of appreciation will also express the meaning of the experience under evaluation. There is thus an important fusion of truth, value, and meaning in Dewey's understanding of the ethics of experience.

But this is not the end of the story. For such an experience must also have a deeply satisfying component. Unless such an emotional level is reached, the willingness to perform such an arduous task over and over again would surely fade. But such feelings of satisfaction do not come merely from instrumental experiences. They are the outcome of what Dewey calls *consummatory* experiences. And this brings us to the relation between ethics and aesthetics. Both are experiential domains and therefore both share the generic traits of experience as such. Experience is rhythmic, organic, corrective, and interactive. So also are aesthetics and ethics.

Feeling, thinking, and doing are terms that capture the entwined presences of ethics and aesthetics. I begin with *feeling*. It is a most significant term. It identifies the basic modality by which we engage the world of experience. It establishes our baseline level of participation within the shifting shapes of the real. How we feel is a direct qualitative index of our experience. It is as fundamental to our way of being in the world as our blood pressure, metabolism and breathing rate. Feeling is the pulse that marks out the rhythms of human existence. It is essentially an axiological reaction to how we are conducting ourselves in the various situations we encounter. Unless we are in touch with these primal feeling states, our power to orientate our life and set goals and directions for ourselves is severely limited.

What we feel in this elementary state is the way in which our situation is affecting us. Dewey's metaphysics paints a portrait of ever-shifting situations that are best understood as fields of experience. These fields contain within themselves focuses that collect and redistribute the energies bound into the situation. Like the positive and negative poles that balance electromagnetic fields, the primary aim of these points of importance is the establishment of balance. The presence of an acceptable level of equilibrium signals the achievement of goodness within a field of experience.

We feel this balance as stability and security. But the feeling is not one of bovine contentment. Rather, the feeling that spreads through a balanced situation is one of live tension generating intense energy for the doings and undergoings that mark experience. It is a sense of controlled excitement that encourages us to investigate the frontiers of new experience. But sometimes this feeling of stability is overthrown by a feeling of dread that signals the presence of the precarious edging into our field of experience. Balance is lost. Equilibrium perishes. Instead of feeling in step with experience, we fall out of phase and find ourselves without direction, energy, or a sense of power. We stand confused in the face of experience and feel stripped of the power to cope. We are at a loss and lost.

Such an experience of imbalance calls for some type of reaction. What we undergo demands a new type of doing—a response that will reconstruct the phases of our experience and bring balance back into the situation. It is the combined responsibility of ethics and aesthetics to carry out such a reconstruction. Neither ethics nor aesthetics is sufficient by itself to restore balance. They must act in concert to restore effective and valuable balance to a situation that has lost its experiential harmony. Feeling plays an essential role in redressing the loss of equilibrium that robs humans of vital energies needed for effective living. The numbness and disillusion that saps much of contemporary culture is due to the loss of energy that results from such confusion. Facing the precarious we retreat to old patterns and play the ostrich. Or we surrender to a sense of boredom and begin to live only for the moment and whatever pleasure might be available. The former is the way of the conservative; the latter is the path of the hedonist. Neither mode of reconstructing experience is effective in the long run. A process universe is always edging into novelty. The conservative must always lose. The hedonist always meets boredom.

There is a false interpretation of this way of dealing with reality that has nothing whatsoever to do with Dewey's fundamental insights into the nature of feeling, doing, and thinking. This ill-informed critique dismisses Dewey's thought (and often the entire tradition of American naturalism and pragmatism) as merely an exercise in fixing things. Pragmatism is simply a dressed-up version of the American penchant for confusing the new with the better. The charge goes, "Nothing matters but progress, progress, and then more progress." The best way to disprove such a shallow interpretation of American philosophy is to understand why it is that Dewey demands that ethics and aesthetics join hands so that the genuine meaning of experience can be had. The word "meaning" is the key to understanding the relation between feeling, thinking, and doing. Life is not about fixing things. It is about experiencing meaning, creating meaning, and sharing meaning. Meaning originates in feeling. If we lack the ability to feel, we lack the capacity to experience meaning. Meaning arises when we sense the difference between what was and what now is. To feel the different is to feel the impact of value within our being. When we are in a position to feel what is coming to be in our environment, we are living on the edge of authentic experience. An experience that makes no difference is not an experience—something must happen.

Dewey's naturalism is a sustained attempt to help us feel the difference that experience makes. In being unalterably opposed to separations of all kinds, Dewey found in his doctrine of feeling and experience the key to overcoming the dualisms that sap the energy of human beings. Such classic dualisms as body and mind, quality and quantity, action and contemplation disappear within the new perspective granted by the category of experience. The universe of our understanding originates in our ability to feel the real presence of vivid experience. The cosmos itself swims in the sea of our feelings just as we swim in its feelings. In the course of our lifetimes, many different types and kinds of feelings arise, but they all share the same trait: every feeling, no matter how joyous, sad, or even boring, has clinging to it an aura of value. Dewey calls this tangible presence a *quale* for it is the quality of the experience that we first of all feel. And what we feel is the difference that the experience makes in our lives. This difference is its value. The feeling of that difference is the source of the meaning we vaguely sense as arising out of our experiences. Feeling, value, and meaning involve each other. Each cannot be reduced to the other but each depends on the other for its experiential reality.

This triad of feeling, value, and meaning runs through all the processes of feeling, doing, and thinking. I want to use this perspective to examine once again Dewey's category of experience. It is his basic way of understanding how nature and ourselves as a part of nature work. It is more fundamental than any other way of dealing with the world. All activities such as feeling, thinking, and doing are at bottom experiences. They share in the generic traits of experience, which include the dimensions of organic interaction, corrective interpretation, and rhythmic temporality. The base line to which philosophy must return is therefore always the same: *experience*.

There are two types of experience, instrumental and consummatory. Ethics deals largely with instrumental experience while aesthetics deals primarily with consummatory experience. I begin with a review of the consummatory. What does Dewey mean by the consummatory? We already know certain things. First, we know that it is a feeling. Second, we know that it arises from some type of interaction with an environment. Third, we know that it makes a specific kind of difference within the field of felt experience. This third dimension holds the key to aesthetic experience. The difference made by an aesthetic experience is that the presence of *a pervasive qualitative whole* is felt throughout its various levels and dimensions.

This sense of wholeness is gained through the ways in which the artist allows the parts of the experience to work together. Instead of separations, one senses a fusion of differences such that the individuality of the parts are respected and made contributors to a growing whole: "The undefined pervasive quality of an experience is that which binds together all the defined elements, the objects of which we are focally aware, making them whole. The best evidence that such is the case is our constant sense of things as belonging or not belonging which is immediate."[8]

The attainment of this wholeness is not a straightforward linear process but rather has its own distinctive rhythm and mode of achievement. Indeed a characteristic of aesthetic experience is that it has no preplanned conclusion beyond that of a consummatory feeling of wholeness. Its completion is neither known in advance nor can it be stipulated beforehand. Aesthetic experience depends on the creativity of the moment as it proceeds toward its completion. But such experience is not a jumble of isolated responses to a situation. Rather, it uses its past in a transfigured way so that *what was* is now part of *what is to be*. Similarly, aesthetic experience invokes the future as a response to what will be when the work is finished. There is in each aesthetic experience a special tempo that marks the rhythm of wholeness as one by one it leads each individual part into an appropriate relation with its others.

This kind of aesthetic achievement is no easy task. It involves the depths of the soul, for resistances arising from either the media used or the subject being developed cannot be dissolved with a flick of the wrist. The artist must do two things at the same time. First, the artist must respect the intractable that is confronted. It is something in its own right and therefore expresses an important value. Perhaps this value may very well be essential for the pervasive qualitative wholeness that is sought. Patience and openness to difference are aesthetic virtues at this point in the creative process. Second, the depths of the artist's soul must be plumbed in order to find the resources needed to carry out the transformation of the different *as different* into a fitting part of the whole. So experience open to the different and experience open to novel depths unplumbed in one's own self fuse together in genuine aesthetic experience.

Art is therefore an experiential dimension existing within the actual conditions of a particular human culture. It is not a set of objects to be placed in a museum or a series of notes to be played for those wealthy enough to purchase a ticket. It is part of the texture of life itself. And insofar as humans are live creatures, they need art in order to live. For art joins form to function, intelligence to action and contemplation to renewal of vision. It cancels out the vicious separations that drain our energies and weaken our resolve to live with more intensity, integrity, wholeness, and depth. We are not just culturally deprived when art has been banished from the public sphere. We are embarking on a path toward death. For with the weakening of experience comes the slow, steady decline of human vitality that eventually brings us face to face with the dissolution of the human.

Intensity, integrity, wholeness, and depth are four normative measures I have used elsewhere in order to estimate the value of natural processes and initiate a reconstruction of environmental ethics.[9] They are also useful in this attempt to formulate the connections between aesthetics and ethics within the tradition of American philosophy. Each norm brings together the ethical and the aesthetic into varying patterns of value. Recalling Dewey's earlier words, these norms describe how the ethical and the aesthetic *belong* to each other so that any ultimate separation of the two is a metaphysical fallacy.

Intensity names the pitch of existence experienced by those involved in the art work. The work brings together artist and perceiver in a new and significantly altered situation. What rises within such a situation is the set of feelings experienced by those committed to participation in it. The difference a work of art makes is the difference in the level of feelings shared by those involved.

Integrity identifies the special ways in which the work of art puts together previously separated dimensions of a particular aesthetic experience. Parts are shown to belong together in such a way as to retain their individuality, but at the same time still contribute in an essential manner to the development of the whole. Also, the contrasts created through these integrations are an especially important part of intensifying the experiences being had.

Likewise, *wholeness* in its rhythmic progression through the varying stages of the artist's creative efforts is a standard always guiding the creation of the work of art. What must be attained at the end of the process is some level of consummatory feeling. The measurement of this experiential dimension involves determining just how well it organizes the energies latent in the creative process. Forms of wholeness express significantly novel ways in which the different and the same belong together. Sometimes this unity is provided by continuity in shape, tone, and color. Other times see this unity expressed through contrasts that emphasize the underlying unity that holds differences together. But no matter what the form, the experience of wholeness always increases the intense feelings had within the aesthetic experience. And, of course, wholeness builds upon whatever forms of integration are already present in the work of art.

Rhythmic continuity is therefore a natural component of this set of normative measures. Intensity demands integration. Integrity anticipates wholeness. *Depth* measures the unexpected resources to be found in the wholeness experienced within the work of art. Just when one believes that one has exhausted all possibilities resident in a particular art work, another dimension reveals itself. Thus depth marks the voluminous presence of possibilities for enriched novel experience lying at the base of the art work. So just as intensity needs integrity and integrity requires wholeness, so also does wholeness need depth if it is to continue to be relevant in the future.

What is consummatory about aesthetic experience is the way in which it sums up and completes what is needed by human beings seeking a fulfilled life. This is also what binds it so forcefully to ethics. Dewey regards ethics as an instrumental experience. This means that the primary emphasis in any ethical deliberation ought to fall upon the method used to achieve the good, resolve a problem, or make sure that good consequences follow from a particular course of action. How is this to be carried out?

We have passed from feeling to thinking. *Thinking* is also an experience but its scope is not as large as that of feeling. For thinking is really the training of intelligence to identify problems and find their solutions. Thus there is always a directed quality to thinking. Its aim is to use its power to find ways and means to achieve ends in view. In fact all effective thinking structures a pattern of inquiry that maps out the boundaries and contents of the problems to be solved. Ethics seeks to determine the most effective procedures to bring about worthy ends. There is therefore a connection between means and ends within the ethical process. In fact, Dewey insists that the only appropriate methodological procedure for ethics is that its ends be brought to mind at the very start of the procedure. This is why Dewey always calls the purposes guiding ethical decisions "ends in view." Identifying and understanding the end is part of the method from the beginning. This does not mean that the end cannot shift during the deliberative process; indeed, such a shift in what one desires is often a beneficial result of naturalistic ethics.

There remain, however, certain specific methodological qualities to be incorporated within ethical experience. In the first place, ethics must assume a scientific dimension and must practice the methods that have proven so successful in our time. This includes adopting a hypothetical stance when viewing goods, values, and the way they are pursued. There is no place for fixed ends in Dewey's philosophy. Naturalism trusts nature which everywhere demonstrates the continual emergence of change, variation, and novelty. To insist on the eternal truth of an ethical principle is to fly in the face of what experience tells us about the shifting nature of the good.

Secondly, those involved in ethical thought must anticipate the rise of different opinions. A search for a single answer is evidence of an unacceptable naïveté in dealing with human nature and character. Also, the boundaries of moral life ought to be broad enough to include all sorts of things not usually connected with ethical deliberation. The growing population of the world is as much a part of a discussion of birth control as the question of the ends of sexual intercourse. Finally, there must be a concentration on the natural needs and ends of human beings. We need a sense of security (both emotional and financial) as much as we need clean air and water. We need the presence of an active community whose interests and aims include our own. We need privacy and we need association. We need to be able to create meaning and share it in our daily life. For Dewey these are not simply political questions. They are profoundly normative ones that are as much a part of ethics as one's honesty and sense of responsibility.

In focusing on the means/end relationship Dewey would have ethics carry out its obligations with the same enjoyment of doubt that characterizes science at its best. Too often, ethics is used to eliminate doubt in matters that are most crucial for the human race. But we know that doubt, disappointment, and confusion are as much a part of life as security and serenity. We naturally shift back and forth between the secure and the precarious and this also occurs within our ethical life. To declare certain problems understood and resolved once and for all by the application of abstract principles is to refuse to use reflective intelligence for the most important issues facing ourselves and others.

This means that ethics is not just the search for the good and the true. It is also about the search for the fair and the fitting. To search for what is appropriate within a particular context is as much of an ethical question as is the effort to determine what is moral and what is immoral. Now I am using "appropriate" here in a very special sense. For "appropriate" stands in for "belonging" and "fitting," two words previously used by Dewey to describe the consummatory. We are now at the last dimension of felt intelligence, doing.

In the pragmatic tradition the act of doing is not synonymous with the skill of fixing what is broken. To do for Dewey is always to grow, but to grow in a most particular way: *To do is to grow in meaning.* This installment of action in the heart of the meaningful is the direct result of the intrinsic relation between value, truth, and meaning. What comes to be in nature is always different from the past. This concept of the perpetual emergence of novelty is the outcome of taking time seriously. There is the possibility of real change and hence real difference when time is seen as an organic component of nature's processes. Now this emergence of the different is also to be understood as the coming to be of value. Value is measured by the intensity of the differences expressing themselves as nature evolves. Thus meaning is the outcome of the differences made by emergent forms of value as they contribute to the onrush of process.

Meaning is therefore brought about by changes in the patterned connections that make up situations. There is a quantitative and qualitative aspect to this emergence of meaning. It can be stated simply:

The more numerous and varied the relations expressing themselves in a particular experience, the more qualitatively intense and integrated are the possible values in that situation.

I say "possible" because it is the agents within the situation that will decide the fate of the growth of meaning in every experience. To act in a Deweyan universe is to establish such connections and patterns of relations in an intense, integrated, holistic, and deep way. When growth in meaning occurs, a new force emerges out of the welter of experience. This novel push towards difference demands its place in the sun. What its destiny will be is dependent on two factors: (1) just how open to forms of difference is the situation; and (2) how well developed in terms of intensity, integrity, wholeness, and depth is this novel growth in meaning.

Meaning either grows or dies. If it grows, it must connect with other meanings in order to establish its own relevance in the world. If it dies, it will be replaced by yet another meaning. In this turbulent scene of shifting meanings, the importance of adding an aesthetic dimension to ethical judgment should be evident. Recall that aesthetic experience is consummatory because it provides a pervasive sense of qualitative wholeness to the doings and undergoings acted on and suffered through in the course of interacting with the environment. It is precisely this sense of a qualitative whole stretching itself between parts and coming to fruition through the acceptance of difference that is essential for any growth in meaning.

Ethical eyesight is too narrow to see all the possibilities relevant in a given set of circumstances. What is needed is that the specific ethical end in view receive some form of expansion so that the horizon of felt values is widened. This is what makes doing a form of growth in meaning. Pragmatism is not some crass search for results that are immediate and selfishly satisfying. It is the search for deeper and more integrated meanings whereby the net that binds together human beings and nature is strengthened at those critical junctions where it threatens to snap. Ethics is not a simple repair job on broken connections. It is much rather the search for wider and deeper connections between human reality and nature. Seen from this perspective, technology is neither a threat in itself nor a golden opportunity. Rather, it gives us one more chance to assess the possibilities of achieving more balanced and integrated relationships.

The ways in which the aesthetic contributes to the ethical and thereby helps establish satisfactory conclusions revolve about the importance of wholeness in the search for the good. It provides a model for the ends in view with which the process of ethical deliberation begins. These ends must always include the factor of wholeness. Ethical judgment that proceeds from airy abstract principles or unreflective codes of behavior has no place in a naturalistic philosophy. Wholeness as a quality to be ever more concretely realized in the process of ethical judgement must make its presence felt at the very beginning. This aesthetic presence establishes a horizon of difference that may beckon a whole solution rather than merely partial ones. In other words the drive towards fixing reality is the exact opposite of what Dewey intends by ethical judgment. What ethics demands is the blending of the instrumental and the consummatory so that both a summing up and a new beginning are experienced within a situation previously out of balance. It is precisely here within this need for a consummatory dimension to ethics that the significance of aesthetics shows itself. Without the sense of wholeness provided by aesthetic experience all ethical judgment quickly degenerates into ad hoc solutions to only partially understood problems. Aesthetics provides the necessary feeling of wholeness that intelligence requires in order to direct its efforts toward instrumentally effective ends in view.

The factor of doing understood as growth in meaning completes this sketch of Dewey's understanding of the relation between ethics and aesthetics. What brings his philosophy together and seals the relation between the ethical and the aesthetic is the central significance of communication as the medium within which meaning grows. What holds a community together are the meanings it shares. The ethical and the aesthetic taken together with growth in meaning form the background against which a community's symbolic code gains the allegiance of its members.

The forms of life that galvanize a community—from its signs of greeting to its gestures of agreement to its educational, economic, and legal institutions—are bound together through their respective allegiances to these shared meanings. This felt presence is expressed through the rising into being of what can be called a "shadow *soma*," a public body in whose gestures of communication we share. A social self arises when we can internalize these embodied signs and repeat them back to others. This public body sets up a felt horizon of meaning against which the drama of the emerging presence of certain types of value is enacted. What happens when new values assert themselves within the onward rush of process? The community can flat out deny their relevance. This is the way of refusal. Or it can roll over and play dead in the face of the newest moment of experience. This is the way of surrender.

The truly effective response involves the creation of new feelings through the growth of the public body, the "shadow *soma*." Our felt forms of communication can make room for new experiences of feeling, thinking, and doing. This reconstructed body of felt gestures, directed intelligence, and patterns of growth expresses the attainment of certain recognized forms of value. But through its hesitations and withdrawals it also expresses the fact that not all values are immediately welcomed. It is by working through these somatic gaps that new values can find their way into the patterns of communal life. Growth in meaning is not primarily a cognitive act. Rather, it is rooted in the wider experience of interaction with the environment. On the most primal level this takes place through the human body. When a public body rises up to provide room for the acceptance of new values, then the real possibility of growth in meaning appears. Such meaning appears gradually: first, within the domain of feeling; second, by means of directed intelligence; and finally, through somatic doing whereby community members can recognize their own feelings in the gestures of their companions. Through the active presence of somatic doing, the path toward the inclusion of difference is made easier. Also, these important episodes in the growth of meaning become more enduring, for these somatic doings eventually become habits within our own personal bodies.

How shall the community react to the different? The measure of the healthy community is to be taken by the degree to which it expands the horizons of its symbolic code so as to incorporate the different into its wholeness of meaning. This is the same as saying that the community must experience difference in a consummatory way. In fact, it is saying that the attitude that can found a great community is an aesthetic one that envisions an ever growing whole even as it respects the individual differences that emerge out of the growth of process. And the key to this transformation is the process of feeling, thinking, and doing which begins with the body and ends with it.

Meaning, truth, and action are the elements of human experience at its best. Traditional Western philosophy has termed these elements the true, the beautiful, and the good. As true, it expresses the carryover of value from the past to the future through the experience of the present. As beautiful, it expresses a level of appropriate fitness between what was, what is, and what will be. As good, it brings to expression the quality of growth that is the sign of human excellence. In this way Dewey naturalizes idealism's insight into the real effectiveness of ideals in guiding human nature and conduct. He achieves this philosophical revolution by reconstructing the relation between aesthetics and ethics. Where once they existed in separate domains, now they work together to unite feeling, thinking, and doing. And the pioneer hefting his ax could sense its fair and fitting presence within the environment. This sense of what belongs and what does not is the focus of Dewey's stress on the central significance of situations in human growth and development.

Inquiry and felt intelligence go together. The initial step in investigating the gaps, separations, and disruptions in experience is first of all to be able to feel what is going on. This depends upon a body that is attuned to its feelings within particular environments. Not all contexts are the same, and to be able to sense the differences within them is the basis of fruitful inquiry. Without a sense for the "feel" of a situation, we are like a ship dead in the water. Once the energy gained from feeling the situation is had, then acts of thinking and doing can take place. But without the gift of felt intelligence, resulting activities are very likely to be off the mark. Proposed solutions can be far more destructive than the problem to be fixed.

Working Connections with Confucius: Li, Yi, and Zhi

I suggest that a primary working connection between Dewey and Confucius is to be found in the concept of *li*.[10] It is to be understood as the equivalent of the felt intelligence that grounds Dewey's concept of inquiry. Also the meaning of *li* must be connected with that of *yi and zhi*. Traditionally, Dewey's concept of inquiry has been understood as merely an extension of the scientific method into the sphere of social, political and personal existence. This is what is behind the labeling of Dewey's thought as just another mode of scientism. But my argument has stressed the underlying aesthetic base of Dewey's sense of human inquiry. It is quite clear that Dewey saw human growth as the deepening of our connections with the world and others. This growth is the outcome of what I have called felt intelligence. Two important consequences follow from this unification of feeling, thinking, and doing known as felt intelligence or inquiry. The instrumental side of Dewey's thought must be judged in terms of its success in bringing human beings into a community of shared meaning. Second, the emotional side of human life must be vividly engaged in acts of inquiry intended to better social existence.

Ames and Rosemont translate *li* as "observing ritual propriety."[11] At first glance, there seems to be an enormous gap between the scientific temper of Dewey's instrumental experience and the Confucian concept of ritual propriety. The key to resolving this problem lies in the term "appropriate." I have used it in the previous chapter to examine the aesthetic depths of Dewey's concept of consummatory experience. By giving it the meaning of "fair and fitting" we get closer to the real meaning of *li* as ritual. Ritual, of course, is to be performed. That is to say, it is to be embodied. It has a fleshly expression and is charged with emotional energy. Further, ritual has a social dimension. Critical to its performance is the fact that others can understand and participate in it. This is precisely what I mean by felt intelligence. One *feels* and *understands* the significance of what is going on.

As Ames and Rosemont put it, "The compass [of *li*] is broad: all formal conduct, from table manners to patterns of greeting and leave-taking, to graduations, weddings, funerals, from gestures of deference to ancestral sacrifices—all of these, and more, are *li*."[12]

Li makes use of the shadow *soma* that arises whenever human beings are in contact with each other. *Li* is the social grammar used by communities to convey their most important values. It is a pattern of unending gestures that communicate meaning and value to a community's members. They are unending because genuine gestures have a symbolic depth that is more or less inexhaustible. In fact when gestures and symbols dry up, the culture is dead. It has fallen into a decline that cannot be reversed except by the violent reconstruction of its symbolic code. Something like this happened in the American Civil War and is happening today in terms of the feminist movement. Dewey was called a "Second Confucius" precisely because he took *li* so seriously. And he was able to do so because of the aesthetic thrust of his thinking.

Confucius lays out the fundamental importance of *li* at the beginning of the twelfth book of the *Analects*:

> Yan Hui inquired about authoritative conduct (*ren*). The Master replied: "Through self-discipline and observing ritual propriety (*li*) one becomes authoritative in one's conduct. If for the space of a day one were able to accomplish this, the whole empire would defer to this authoritative model. Becoming authoritative in one's conduct is self-originating—how could it originate in others?"
>
> Yan Hui said, "Could I ask what becoming authoritative entails? The Master replied, "Do not look at anything that violates the observance of ritual propriety (*li*); do not listen to anything that violates the observance of ritual propriety (*li*); do not speak about anything that violates the observance of ritual propriety (*li*); do not do anything that violates the observance of ritual propriety (*li*)."
>
> "Though I am not clever," said Yan Hui, "allow me to act on what you have said."[13]

Notice Yan Hui's response: he will *act* on this advice. He will not just trust his cleverness. Hypocrisy is often the stepchild of cleverness and it is this attitude of intentional deceit that Confucius despises. It is at this point that *yi* and *zhi* become important. *Yi* signifies the sense of what is fitting and appropriate. It is akin to what at the end of the first chapter I termed beauty, that is, the fair and the fitting. To act consistently in such a manner demands openness to what is happening. It is the very opposite of the narcissism that infects so much of Western culture. The disciples of Confucius noticed this as his primary character trait:

> There were four things that the Master abstained from entirely: he did not speculate, he did not claim or demand certainty; he was not inflexible, and he was not self-absorbed.[14]

Yi demands attention to the nuances of the situation so that what is unbalanced can be reformed. *Yi* is absolutely necessary in bringing about the achievement of becoming human (*ren*):

> The Master said, "To fail to cultivate excellence (*de*), to fail to practice what I learn, on coming to know what is appropriate (*yi*) in the circumstances to fail to attend to it, and to be unable to reform conduct that is not productive—these things I worry over."[15]

Yi's correlative relation to *li* lies in its power to remind us that gestures and symbols are only useful if they direct us toward what is fair and fitting. Not every gesture is appropriate. The *yi* of *li* involves deft discernment. As a mode of communication, acts of *li* must fit into the context in which they are used:

> The Master said, "Exemplary persons in making their way in the world are neither bent on nor against anything; rather they go with what is appropriate (*yi*).[16]

Above all else, *yi* entails participation. Just as Dewey saw experience as the way in which the different could come to be included in human culture in a fair and fitting way, so also Confucius demands that his disciples actually take part in what is happening. There is no such thing as a spectator theory of knowledge. *Yi* means involvement. Only then can what is appropriate show itself. This knowing is a result of direct experience. It is not a rigid set of rules to be followed no matter what the circumstances. The world is always in the throes of a creative push toward the different. At its finest, human culture ought to be prepared to deal with these ever-evolving situations. This is both the meaning and the test of one's grasp of *yi* as cultural force. It is also the meaning and test of felt intelligence.

Zhi means to know in the sense of bringing into reality the meaning of a situation. Since thought by itself is but one level of the process of felt intelligence, there must be other dimensions to the act of knowing. *Zhi* names the process whereby we realize both the existence and the value of what is known. By internalizing the embodied intelligence that grasps what is really going on, we take on the character of the reality we claim to know. In this way feeling, thinking and doing unite to uncover the core values embedded in life's situations. The Confucian insistence on a real continuity between thought and action underlies this way of understanding the relation between the fair, the fitting, the appropriate, the true, and the real. Again as Ames and Rosemont maintain, "If to finalize is to make final and to personalize is to make personal, then to realize must mean to make real. . . ."[17]

The sense of immersion in situations so as to provide productive advice and counsel is caught in these words of Confucius:

> The Master said, "Do I possess wisdom (*zhi*)? No, I do not. But if a simple peasant puts a question to me, and I come up empty, I attack the question from both ends until I have gotten to the bottom of it."[18]

Perseverance, persistence, participation in the actual situation at hand—all these strengths are involved in the Confucian concept of inquiry. The correlation between *li*, *yi*, and *zhi* mirrors that which is brought together in the concept of felt intelligence. This does not suggest that we make up the truth. Nor does it claim feeling to be the ground of objectivity. Dewey and Confucius are not advocating a type of rampant subjectivity or a bloodless objectivity. What they are arguing for is a kind of thinking that stresses the act of discernment as the primary goal of philosophy as a cultural endeavor. All cultures are normative in the sense that they advocate what they think is best for their members. What has made this task so difficult in the present day is that the circle that surrounds the members of our culture now includes all members of the planet, all sentient beings, as well as the total environment. Never has normative thinking been more necessary.

Contemporary speculative philosophy bears witness to the growing importance of bringing together thought and action.[19] This development parallels Dewey's insistence on the significance of action as a mode of understanding. Also there is the Neo-Confucian tradition that stresses the fact that understanding follows upon action. The works of Chu-Hsi and Wang-yang Ming use the doctrine of the unity of thought and action as pivots for their commentaries on Confucian thought.[20] When these concepts are read in the light of Dewey's insistence on the continuity between means and ends, the value of harmonizing thought, feeling, and action is made evident. Reconstruction of *li* as the ground of global philosophy is a necessary step in the process of humanizing materialistic culture.

A fitting conclusion to this chapter is to be found in the words of Confucius:

> Zilu inquired about consummate persons. The Master replied, "Persons who are as wise as Zang Wuzhong, as free from desires as Bian Zhuangzi, and as cultivated as Ranyou, and who in addition, have become refined through observing ritual propriety (*li*) and playing music (*yue*)—such persons can be said to be consummate. But," he continued, "need consummate persons of today be all of this? If on seeing a chance to profit they think of appropriate conduct (*yi*), on seeing danger they are ready to give their lives, and when long in desperate straits, they still do not forget the words they live by—such persons can also be said to be consummate.[21]

3

Culture

Values and Situations

Western philosophy is characterized by its effort to identify those irreducible elements that lie at the base of reality. Thus Plato formulated his theory of ideas and Aristotle had his doctrine of substance and accidents. Dewey's version of this search for the generic traits of existence is his insistence that a fundamental event resides at the core of all experience. He calls it a "situation." It is a unifying thread that pulls together the many dimensions of his philosophy.

Every situation is unique because it has a special spatiotemporal spread that establishes its date and place. This means that within each situation there is a defining character that arises from the way in which this particular field of experience has come to be. Furthermore, this quality is the outcome of the situation's power to unify in an organic way the different parts of its pattern of being. There is both an identity and a difference to be found in each situation and it is the quality of their distribution that determines the value of the situation. The first chapter discussed these elements as the interplay of sameness and difference.

Situations are not static, for each has its own special rhythmic signature. The development of a situation proceeds through varying phases and parts. There is no single right way for a situation to be. Each has its own way of being and part of the art of human life is to have the sensitivity to spy out the special structure that marks each and every situation. What diversifies each situation is the way in which the various dominant poles in its field of activity influence each other. This is never a straightforward influence, for a situation is almost always complex. There is rarely one single cause needing identification, but rather a myriad set of interactive influences that flow together to make up the dynamics of the situation. Understanding a situation requires exceptional deftness—a kind of feel for the situation that lets its process come forward and reveal itself in all its rich concreteness.

For example, consider a family about to receive a visit from an in-law. The situation calls for a reinterpretation of the family's experience based on its past history with that in-law. Furthermore, each member of the family has something to contribute to the situation (and, of course, something that may very well detract from it). There will be no simple solution as to how to handle this situation, but certain guidelines based on past experience and future expectations can be set forth. Nevertheless, these are just guidelines. How the teenagers will use these standards to shape their behavior will differ markedly from the younger siblings and from the parents themselves. Also the "in-lawed" relative will have an entirely different perspective. The various poles within this situational field will each have their say and influence the others.[1] A situation is therefore much more like a work of art than a simple diagram of physical forces.

To understand a situation and resolve it in a favorable manner requires aesthetic sensitivity to the forces at play within its boundaries. These energies are best brought to a consummatory conclusion by coaxing a quality of wholeness out of its varying parts, dimensions, and rhythms. This resolving force is felt in a noncognitive manner, for experience is first of all a matter of "feel." The feel for a situation is brought about by a wise sense of what forces are at play within it, what sort of creative resolution lies within its structure, and what outcomes are possible within the doings and undergoings involved in this concrete set of conditions. To say that experience is a great teacher is to acknowledge the ways in which past situations have been successfully resolved. Wisdom is the result of paying attention to experience insofar as it guides us into more satisfactory relations with our environment. What is gained is a sense of completion that unites what was once separate and brings together what was once divided. Aesthetically felt, wisdom expresses in the fullest manner possible the sense of true belonging characterizing authentic consummatory experience.

Wholeheartedness replaces the conflicted responses that define experience lived without an enduring sense of what is important in a given situation.

Situations are marked by extremes of tensions that are the result of the various pushes and pulls seeking resolution within them. These tensile nodes set up the polarities through which a situation first expresses itself, then experiences its lack of unity, and then, where and when possible, resolves these feelings into a satisfactory whole. The feelings generated within these polar fields are what account for the sense of being in phase and out of phase that is part of every situation. The shifting balances within every situation establish a dynamic stability as well as a definite sense of the precarious. It is these alternating rhythms that set up the feel of a situation. True wisdom involves the ability to feel these shifting phases and respond to them in such a way as to bring forth whatever wholeness is possible within a given situation. This is the real meaning of Dewey's concept of directed intelligence. The instrumental converts into the aesthetic as soon as wholeness becomes the goal of human culture. In the end there is no hard and fast line between the instrumental and the aesthetic. In fact, the major task of instrumental inquiry is the transformation of experience into aesthetic consummations. Once again: *No more separations!*

Every situation is situated at the axis of a background and a foreground. The background is made up of all those sources of funded experience that in the past have proven effective in leading human beings towards growth in wholeness. In short, the background is made up of the cultural aims and pursuits that foster the values cherished by society. The foreground is the specific concrete situation itself. This set of conditions constitutes the actual spread of values seeking resolution into ever more growing modes of wholeness. This foreground requires the most careful analysis, for it expresses the synthesis of past, present, and future experience as had in the immediate moment. The feelings aroused by the situation are indicative of the vast flow of values that actually makes up this set of conditions. It is by varying the foreground of the actual situation with the background of the cultural matrix that alternatives for developing patterns of wholeness can be glimpsed. Imagination is not idle fantasy. It is essential for the growth of wholeness as a real factor in experience.

When imagination effectively plays over a situation, there looms forth a focus area that appears to sum up and express in a very intense manner what the situation is all about. This focus is the place from which the varying meanings of the situation will assert themselves as the situation moves toward a successful resolution. This explains why artists are the true experimenters, since they must be willing to abandon one failed course for the sake of a more promising one. Thus aesthetics and the resolution of situations are mutually related whenever the question of achieving wholeness of experience is at issue.

There are three phases in the development of a situation. It begins when that which was once in equilibrium now fails to sustain balance. This is followed by various changes in behavior that seek to reestablish balance among the values in the situation. This is the phase of experimentation. If and when this search for an alternative succeeds, there then results a renewed sense of balance—an achievement signaling the resolution of the situation. The conclusion to a successfully resolved situation is always the same: the experience of new meaning. This novel consequence is the expression of a distinctively different quality felt throughout the situational field. What began as a lack of belonging culminates in a new sense of what is most appropriate and fitting in the situation. Feelings emerge out of a situation and are its driving forces. Dewey maintains that we feel these feelings even before we have had a chance to think about them. Therefore, every situation is a royal road to authentic experience. It establishes a vast domain of noncognitive experience that is brimming with value and significance. We experience the relations active within a situation before we know them. This sets up a field of experience that is both the foundation and the source of future feelings, knowings, and doings. The reason why aesthetics becomes the paradigm discipline for Dewey (and all other American philosophers working in the tradition of pragmatic naturalism) should now be clear. It is only through the acquisition of a deft sensibility that the full resources of experience can be put at our disposal. It is aesthetics that can lead us into fruitful contact with this primordial field of feelings lying at the base of reality. When one recognizes that every situation has an orientation, a goal and a particular location, then the importance of aesthetic sensibility becomes even more evident. How else is one to feel the drift of a situation if one is not attuned to its tacit orientation? The in-laws' visit is not about economic theories, political ideologies, or theories of knowledge. Its fundamental problematic is about bringing together two very different spheres of values in a way that can allow each to grow in understanding of the other. Failure to sense the fundamental orientation of a situation can lead to the most catastrophic blunders. Furthermore, each situation has within it an unformed but influential goal—a way of resolving the unbalancing strife characterizing its field of relations. To act without a feeling for this goal, no matter how dim or vague, is to invite disaster. Finally, every situation is also a concrete event that has its own place and date. Grasping these modes of location is essential for understanding the special structure of feelings had within that particular situation. There is no such thing as a general situation. Each has its own orientation, goal, and location. There is only *this* situation or *that* situation.

But how specifically can one grasp the feel of a situation if one does not already know it? The answer is to be found in the real presence of the shadow soma discussed in the previous chapter. This public body is what allows humans to enter into attuned relations with the feelings aroused by situations. I also call it the "habitual body" because it is governed by the cultural habits ingrained in our way of experiencing the world. These habits are the ways in which a world of continuity is established in the face of the onward rush of process. I greet each person I meet by extending my hand. Each person is different but the gesture of openness remains constant throughout all the meetings of my day. Furthermore, this gesture is noncognitive. I do it without thinking about it. But—and this is key—it is filled with meaning. It is embodied intelligence. For my open hand expresses a meaning understood by others as well as myself. Our culture has shown us how to do this in an unthinking yet meaningful way. The acquisition of these powers of the habitual body is the first great task of any human being's growth from infancy to adulthood. I must be able to embody the rituals, actions, and gestures of my culture. Without this capacity I will move through the world as a silent figure unable to interact with or influence those with whom I dwell. It is through the fact that I share a habitual body with my fellow citizens that I can communicate.

This act of fleshed thought incarnates the meaning of those values that are significant for a given culture. I feel the presence of those values without ever knowing them in a strictly cognitive fashion. This is what Dewey means by the aesthetic dimension and what I mean by "felt intelligence." It is that region of experience and value that lies at the bedrock level of each and every situation. Its presence is felt before it is known and the way in which we know it is through the deftness of our habitual body, an organ of attunement created by our culture so that members of society can share the feelings that make up their world.

Situations always begin with a premonition of the precarious nature of our existence. Cultural habits provide structures of stability with which to face the sense of insecurity pervading the environment. The habitual body lays down lines of effective responses that have proven their past worth in reconstructing our experience. Habits embody the principles of action that bring about the creation of important values. Habits become habits because they have proved their worth in the past; consequently, their failure to deliver the response we desire signals the onset of significant social distress. The failure of the habitual body to right what appears to be going wrong tells the community that its way of life is in peril.

Furthermore, since habits are not single, separate responses but entire repertoires of entwined ways of dealing with environmental threats, the failure of one habit suggests that the structure of the public mind itself needs repair. For what habits provide are vectors of response to the breakdown of previously satisfactory modes of experience. Habits take from the acquired wisdom of the community those forms of energetic response that have proved effective in past crises and apply them to present difficulties. They were analyzed in the last chapter as examples of what Confucius calls *li*. When they no longer work, a double threat looms on the public horizon. One threat involves our understanding of the past, for quite obviously our previous grasp of its meaning is now proving false. The other threat is in the immediate present, for we are left without an adequate understanding of the contours of our present experience. When habits fail, the roof falls in on our accustomed ways of dealing with the world. Great cracks appear in the walls of our publicly shared house of understanding.

What usually ensues is a kind of cultural paralysis that often turns toward the search for a scapegoat. The perceived fact that "They" did it becomes a way of simultaneously working off anxiety and purifying the community of whatever curse has befallen it. Of course such ignorance never works and the community is plunged into an even deeper crisis when these modes of adjustment fail. What is called for is a reconstruction of the community's understanding of its experience. It must revise its symbolic code and along with it, the habits formerly used to structure its way of dealing with the world. The community must reinvent the ways in which it participates in experience.

Participation is the key word in this process of rebuilding community in the face of situations that overwhelm it. Societies that run away from crises perish when the crises do not go away. Likewise, societies that merely try to apply bandages to social cuts and bruises are whistling in the dark. The fact is that the failed responses of the habitual body announce a general breakdown in the effectiveness of our way of being in the world. This is because the habits used to negotiate both the stable and the precarious poles of experience are themselves the result of long-tested experience. It must be remembered that to have a structure is to participate in a value which itself then becomes a norm for that which is structured. The circle binding values, actions, and meanings is a closed one. Failed action signals a failed value. Signs, symbolic codes, and rituals of social action are not external to the situation within which they have application. They *are* the situation. A failure of one aspect of the habitual body will echo through all its other responses. The vitality of the public mind has been weakened and all its embodied actions will show a similar loss of strength and focus. A general ineffectiveness will settle on the community in question and its capacity to respond in experientially meaningful ways will be seriously diminished. This is all due to a simple law of experience that Dewey laid down a long time ago. Experience requires direct participation in the doings and undergoings of community life. Anything that skirts this responsibility or shunts it off to one side will perish of its own lack of reality. The only thing that can correct misunderstood experience is better understood experience.

Direct experience is the best medicine. Another way to put this is to state categorically that every community ought to have an all-important rule: in all situations of any kind whatsoever, its primary duty is to *learn*. But once again, learning does not here mean some form of "fix-it" thinking. We are not talking about the forms of false instrumentalism that have given Dewey's philosophy such a bad name. What is needed is the effort to discover forms of qualitative wholeness that can reconstruct situations. If and when a balanced satisfaction is reached, a renewed sense of equilibrium moves through the community and its general posture towards its problems is remarkably altered. New ways of adapting are found, new sources of energy are felt, and new modes of understanding are expressed throughout public life.

When the body is used as the real ground of social participation, a type of learning takes place that is both broadly based and deeply anchored in the emotional life of the community. Culture is never a matter of merely learning how to decode the signals of others. Such ways of fitting in reveal their shallowness almost immediately when crises affect community life. What happens when the habitual body takes up the act of learning is the establishment of a vital field of action—a region is cleared within which both the sufferings and the accomplishments of humans bonded together in experience can be shared. Learning takes place on the widest and deepest available scale. The attuned habitual body conducts its citizens into ways of behavior that consolidate the gains made by new modes of reconstructing situations.

These acts of significant experience move the community towards levels of fulfillment not previously guessed at. And the habits that rise in the wake of this reconstruction of experience are the community's way of gaining a broad level of security for its future interactions with the world. They, too, may fail in the future, but another learning experience has taken place. Such possibilities for renewed learning are really all that human beings can ask for in a universe marked by uncertainty, impermanence, and failure. The habits now secured are once again experienced as ways in which the community's newly acquired ends in view are brought into play. And the reconstructed habitual body that results from these new habits becomes a field of dynamically felt expressions of meaning. It is this field of meaning that is at the core of every culture's invitation to experience its most important meanings and values. The habits achieved by working through situational crises also extend their power to other dimensions of the community's life. This enactment of an embodied public mind is what ultimately grants authority and effectiveness to any culture's attempt to secure the allegiance of its members. Pure rational knowing shrinks in significance when faced with the power of directly experienced expressive meaning. It is to this reservoir of felt value that Dewey directs our attention if we would understand how a culture shapes its values and nourishes its citizens.

Situations are the basic structures of our experience. Through them we are bonded to reality and to each other. Each situation has some level of content that needs both understanding and reconstruction. Such an inquiry involves the field of action set up by the various poles of value operating throughout the situation's region of influence. A concrete understanding of the situation must also take into account its varied rhythms of development. For within every situation there are protagonists at play seeking their rightful due. It is only by recognizing these tensions that potential forms of wholeness can be imagined. This will require the full force of the human body, both its emotional depths and its cultural refinements, acting so as to establish a felt region of experienced meaning for the community. Fringe and horizon, foreground and background, perspective and ends in view must all be given an influential role in this drama of enacted meaning. What is needed most of all is that sense of art that can generate a free flowing movement of the whole throughout the situation in question. In a word, what is required is communication, or as Confucius would call it, li.

It is important to understand that for Dewey all situations are potentially aesthetic. I contribute the following and ask readers to draw their own conclusions.

"The Catch"

I met Yuri when he was six years old. He was frightened by what had been happening in his life. But he did not show this fear. Instead he put on a tough face and demanded his place in the world. His mom and dad had recently concluded an unhappy divorce. In addition he had been born in Holland, had an infancy beset with difficulties, and was still adjusting to life in America. And to top it all off, he was decidedly small for his age. I became a surrogate parent since he was the son of the woman I was living with.

Such was Yuri when he came to live in my house in the late fall. One day when I was idly throwing a baseball in the air his mom said, "Hey, Yuri, Joe can teach you baseball; he's good at it." I looked at him and he stared back at me quizzically. I learned much later that he had always wanted to learn how to play baseball but his efforts had been thwarted. His mom did not really know how and his dad, a native of Holland, was superb at soccer but knew little about American baseball.

We left things there but a week later I met him in a park and he had a baseball and a glove with him. So began the experience of Yuri, Joe, and baseball. I asked him if he wanted to play. He said, "Yes." So I tossed him a little pop fly and he ran under it. Instead of catching the ball, he was hit right in the face by it. He was stunned by the impact of the ball and I am sure his nose was hurting. But he did not back off. He went after the dropped ball, threw it back and waited for another one. This did not surprise me because there are basically two types of ball players: those who go after the ball and those who run away from it. Yuri was not going to run away and hide. In fact he caught the next one and the next one and the next one. We spent the day throwing the ball to each other. Long, lazy throws that arched their way to his glove through *the late fall sky. Without a word being said, both of us understood that a new experience had begun. We were no longer wary of each other, he scoping me to find out what kind of adult I was going to be and I trying to figure how to deal with this new addition to my household.*

Now we had something to do. Something we could feel and something we could think about. The Maine winter came on and all through the ice, hail, snow, and cold, we played baseball. That's right! We went outside to the barren parking lot behind the house and there in the face of the bitter wind, I pitched wiffle balls to him and he learned how to bat. Every outing concluded with me throwing a number of very high fly balls way over his head. He didn't catch all of them but he made several spectacular plays. One I remember involved his falling into a snowbank as he snagged a particularly difficult fly ball.

When spring came, we began to play some Bronx games. In particular, we played off-the-wall and stickball. I remember one especially thrilling game of off-the-wall where we played for seventy-six innings until he finally won it on a crucial error by me. Stickball gave him his first chance to deal with hard line drives hit right at him and to his left and right. He immediately sensed the way the ball would hook or fade or dive. He was a natural. He loved baseball like I do. We played for hours, every day right through the summer.

This experience cemented a friendship. It was the soil out of which our relationship grew. All the issues of parenting and child rearing were experienced in a different light because of baseball and what it meant to him and me. Of course, it did not solve everything and there were many, many rough moments during the next five years. But through it all, it was baseball that became the situation within which we found solutions to our problems.

Five years later, I found myself standing behind the outfield fence in left center field. I was watching Yuri's team play the last innings of a Little League All Star game. He was playing center field and his team was holding onto a slim lead as the final innings progressed. The other team had the bases loaded and was threatening to score. It was a hot June evening. Swarms of gnats floated up into faces and the mosquitoes were having a feast. It felt like the air was on fire. No wind. Absolute stillness. There was a sullenness in the sky.

Then the batter swung. He put an incredible lick on a fastball and it was coming right at me as I stood behind the outfield fence. It was home run time and I was going to catch the ball. Suddenly as I prepared to try to catch it, I caught a dark shadow entering my field of vision. It didn't seem like anything but it was enough to distract me for a moment. I concentrated on regaining my sight of the flight of the ball. It was extremely hard hit, a bullet about five feet off the ground and rising. The players were frozen on the basepaths. The large crowd had caught its collective breath. Sullen skies and a silent ball park. Then out of nowhere Yuri loomed directly into my field of vision. He had run from dead center field where he was playing and had just launched himself into the air. He was at least five feet off the ground and his body was stretched to its full limit as the ball thudded into his glove. The sound was awful. It was mean. The ball struck the leather with tremendous force. Everyone in the park must have heard the smack. Yuri fell to the ground holding onto the ball. Then he rolled over and flipped the ball to the left fielder. The crowd found its voice and began to cheer. He had made the consummate catch of his still young lifetime.

Now that was an experience.

❀

The act of communication is a work of wonder for Dewey. He never ceases to be amazed by the fact that it happens at all. He considers it the central mystery of social life. This is quite a reaction from a thinker most often branded as a dyed-in-the-wool materialist who overprizes science as the best means for understanding human life. But there are good reasons why Dewey would consider communication a miraculous event. After all, how does it happen that one human being can actually understand another? What allows meanings to be shared among different people? And how is it that these acts multiply until they become the bonds that bring together entire communities of human beings?

Remember that for Dewey what human beings learn first are not facts but meanings. Humans acquire the knowledge of facts by means of a highly abstract process that is grounded in a disciplined detachment from immediate experience. Meaning, on the other hand, comes about through an active involvement in full experience. This experiential process is rooted in the strivings and undergoings that mark authentic interaction with the environment. The experience of meaning results from being involved in concrete situations. Meaning arises when the difference between what was and what now is can be expressed. This measure of a difference in a situation is the outcome of the various ways in which its components are rearranged so as to culminate in a more balanced and satisfying conclusion.

In effect meanings emerge when the values involved in one set of circumstances give way to new ones. This reconstruction takes place by reason of shifts and alterations in the way in which the events in question are experienced. The dreaded in-laws turn out to be not so bad after all. "Meaning" is therefore the word that best describes the emergence of new forms of value that emerge from the process of becoming. In a phrase, the discovery of meaning is simultaneously the recognition of the presence of a real difference in our lives. If what occurs makes no difference, then what occurs, quite literally, is meaningless. And as meaningless it is also useless, for it has no bearing on the situation in question. The connection between experience and value, meaning and difference is an intimately coherent one. The full understanding of one term requires a necessary reference to the others. An experience that does not make a difference is a contradiction in terms. A value that does not alter the contemporary situation is not a value, for it makes no difference. And what lacks meaning does so because it cannot be experienced as different from its predecessors or contemporaries.

It lies in the nature of meaning that it be shared. Meanings that cannot be shared are meaningless. The connection between meaning and sharing is as tight as that between meaning and difference. Better put, meaning must not only be shared, it must also be participated in. We must inhabit meaning if its full significance is to illuminate regions of experience. This brings us to the question of expression. What does not make a difference cannot be expressed. But what does make a difference has already expressed itself in some way or other. Great communities are founded on their power to recognize the presence of such differences and give them full and adequate expression. In fact, the culture of any community is the record of its successes and failures in bringing to expression its most important values. Cultures are the sum of their acts of communication. How they identify what is important and convey those meanings to their members is the ultimate test of their worthiness. All cultural acts from gestures of politeness to works of art are expressive media through which the values of a culture are made public and shared.

In creating itself, a culture brings to concrete expression what it considers important. Culture is not about pretty things or the treasures of the rich. It does not exist in museums or galleries or theaters or books. It is in fact the ongoing process of finding adequate media for the expression of values important to a community and its people. The Irish stepdance differs from the tango but neither is given true recognition when they are dismissed as mere folk art. A culture that cannot communicate its meanings is on the way out. All colonizers know this and that is why they first attack the art forms of a community. If one can wipe out the modes of expression, sharing, and communication used by a culture, one has also effectively wiped out its public mind. It becomes a mindless entity ripe for any sort of exploitation, from slavery to consumer capitalism.

Social interaction is made impossible when the forms of expression in a given community are allowed to stiffen and die. For community is not only about expressing the values one upholds; it is also about participating in the lives of others. How can I share the meaning of love, service, generosity, and bravery if I cannot witness it in the lives of others? How can these others find these traits in me if I cannot express them in my own life? A community is formed when its members can identify, share, and express something in common. In fact that is the original meaning of the Greek word for "community," *Koinonia*. This something in common must be expressed through forms of participation if a genuine community is to arise. Once again, the theme of belonging asserts itself. It is a template that measures successful action within the structures of experience. Likewise, it is the standard for judging the good resolution of situations. And finally, it is the normative measure for estimating the development of healthy individuals and communities.

Belonging becomes such a crucial concept because to belong is to take part in, to share, and to contribute. Each of these three dimensions of lived human experience—participating, sharing, and belonging—provides a rich perspective summing up Dewey's major ideas on the meaning of human life. When I participate in the life of the community, I must do so through some type of media by which I can gain access to the feelings, thoughts, and values of my fellow human beings. I have called this medium the "shadow soma" and the "habitual body." This public body is long in the making and it holds in its history the formation of the consciousness of the community. It is the reservoir that keeps the memories of the community. Its long history is a record of the successes and failures experienced since the time of its coming into being. It holds available the successful habitual responses to troublesome situations that the community has used in its lifetime. Its body memory contains the essential gestures whereby community members recognize each other's needs and desires. Finally and most importantly, it is the place where the normative measures used by the community are kept safe.

I have stressed before the importance of seeing philosophy as a discipline devoted to normative thinking. A community that lacks the loving pursuit of wisdom also lacks defining standards for its cultural acts of communication. Without a practiced art of normative thinking the community is bereft of meaning, for there is no way to measure out the difference made by authentic experience. The meaning of value is directly related to the difference that it makes. If such differences go unremarked because of a lack of normative measures, then the community has descended into the dark waters of nihilism. Even relativism would be a better fate, for at least that way of thinking is based on some type of standard. For what else does "relative" mean than relative to something? Thus the first way in which belonging is experienced in a healthy and growing community is through direct participation in the body public that arises within the shared experience of community. An individual belongs to a community by participating in the generalized felt awareness that makes up its enduring background of value and meaning.[2] To participate always involves an act of normative thinking whereby we share the awareness of values held by our fellow community members.

Sharing takes place through finding ways of communicating that encourage experiences different from our own. Sharing therefore concerns the way in which difference is brought into the sphere of customary experience. It is precisely at this juncture that the real merit of aesthetic experience once again reveals itself. To bring what is different into my experience demands in the first place an extraordinary act of generosity. Recall that experience oscillates between the stable and the precarious. For the most part our desires tend toward the safe and the secure. Danger may be a thrill but it also destroys any sense of inner peace. To incorporate the different within my accustomed way of life risks upsetting the balance I have struggled to achieve. What can move me to actions that would put in peril my hard-won organization of experience? It is the promise of greater wholeness and more intense satisfaction. But this is precisely what is promised at the outset, during and at the end of aesthetic experience. The consummatory nature of experience is not achieved only at the end of the aesthetic process. Rather it is present at the very start. It generates the desire to go further, the energy to risk more, and the inspiration to grow in deeper and richer experience. Furthermore, it is present as a guiding force throughout the various stages of development that are always part of

the aesthetic process. At the end of the process, the consummatory satisfaction so intensely experienced is seen to have been within the
entire experience from the very start.

The feeling that is so effective in driving the aesthetic process
forward toward its completion is the sense of qualitative wholeness
that pervades the entire experience. What is longed for is a deeper and
wider sense of wholeness. It is this desire for a more complete experience that encourages the risk taking involved in upsetting the stable
relations marking our lives. The promise of an incipient wholeness
encourages us to recognize the fact that there must be a place for difference in our lives. To be whole is to let difference find its place
within the identity of a whole. Wholes that have no difference in their
parts are really not wholes. They are mere simples expressing unalter-
able sameness. They live by means of refusing difference. Likewise,
parts that lack a unifying force are mere aggregates. They are not
wholes. To be a whole is always to be more than the sum of parts.

This "more than" is what powers aesthetic experience. Another
name for wholeness is openness, and this width of welcome is precisely
what difference needs if it is to become part of our experience. Therefore when issues of sharing are at stake, the proper path ought to
involve the aesthetic dimensions of experience. It is only there that
room for difference is a required part of the entire experiential project.
The "more than" characterizing aesthetic experience signifies the
ready acceptance of difference into an enlarged form of wholeness. In
this way, what does not originally belong finds its own unique and sin-
gular place within the structure of the whole.

The power to contribute is the third and final feature of Dewey's
idea of belonging. There is a commonly held conviction that the community will swallow up individuality and generate a gray, faceless, and
bureaucratic social facade. Or often, the converse is held to be the
truth, namely, that strong and radical individuality will upend a community's goals and plans. Neither idea really understands Dewey's
insight into the importance of grounding value within the aesthetic
dimensions of experience. When it comes to aesthetic experience,
everything depends upon the individuality of those involved in the situation, for we experience the aesthetic from the depths of our own personal being. If we lack the creative sensitivity to see into a work of art
and sense its importance, then the community will be bereft of a significant source of values. Likewise, true individuality does not reside in

the exotic or the bizarre. To exhibit difference merely for the sake of difference is the lowest grade of creativity. The fully live individual naturally seeks to share experience so that communication can intensify the insights won through the hard work of aesthetic perception. Thus the healthy community depends on the ingenuity and sensitivity of its members for its continuing growth. Without strong individuals, the community's capacity to uncover novel meaning is undermined. A mood of impoverished awareness steals over the community and its art forms soon degenerate into the sterile act of decoding symbols.

To contribute means to express one's own individuality as it relates to the sense of wholeness suffused throughout the aesthetic experience. Communities terrified by individuality do themselves no service, for such fear chokes off the very source of meaning and value needed to make a difference. Like all situations, the relation between an individual and the community creates a field of action displaying shifting nodes of importance. These poles are not antagonists but rather hold each other together by reason of the force that develops between them. Struggle is no sign of failure. It is much rather an indication that something of great significance is happening.

This perspective also accounts for Dewey's insistence on the importance of democracy.[3] His confidence in this form of government flows from his trust in the natural rightness of including all types of individuals in the community's quest for wholeness. Bonded in meaning and sharing the same public body, the great community is marked by the exceptional intensity of its cultural life. Dewey provides a simple but profound formula that overcomes the old and tired dispute between the partisans of individual freedom and the advocates of strong community action. The formula reads, "The more fruitful and varied the relations in a community, the stronger and more intense its experience." The individual need not fear being swallowed up by the community because the community needs the special gifts that only authentic individuality can offer. Seeing fruitless conflict between the individual and the community as inevitable is a fallacy built on bad metaphysics and an even worse aesthetics.

In terms of communal life there is no ultimate divide between the individual and the group. Aesthetics is grounded on the act of feeling but it is always a unique type of feeling. This mode of feeling is a sense of the underlying pervasive whole that can be potentially worked out within the aesthetic act itself. Now human feeling is dependent upon depth of character, for only an individual person can feel in powerfully aesthetic ways. This means that the capacity to feel is in direct proportion to the sensibility possessed by the individual. Without strength of individual character, no great intensity of experience is really possible. The same can be said about the depths of creativity needed by the community to bridge the differences it will inevitably meet as it grows and develops. Creativity is the gift of imagining the different. Reflected in every act of aesthetic creativity is a unique particularity that springs from the individuality of those involved in the experience. The community depends upon the human individual. It draws upon the individual's unique character in order to tap into the reservoir of feelings that makes growth in qualitative wholeness possible.

The act of belonging is not exhausted by membership in a single community. There are many communities—familial, religious, economic, educational, and political—that require our participation. But in each instance the key to effective belonging lies in how well we can share with others the values that we cherish. The reason for this lies in the deepest dimension of human experience. Above all else, we human beings need to continue to grow. And human growth can only be measured through the ways in which novel and different meanings become incorporated in our individual and communal lives. Communication is not a luxury. It is a human necessity as important for our existence as clean air, water, and nourishing food.

Dewey uses the term "associated life" to sum up what he means by the relation between sharing meanings, building a community, and good human growth and development. Remember that Dewey's fundamental mission was to restore a sense of wholeness and continuity to human experience and culture. *No more separations.* This means that relations between events are as real and as important as the events themselves. Earlier I called these relations feelings. This identification of feelings with relations is the key to unlocking the working connection between Dewey's theory of reality and philosophy of culture. What lies at the heart of Dewey's naturalism is the conviction that relations can be felt with immense intensity and qualitative wholeness. And this power to feel relations is concrete evidence that reality is made up of sets of events whose fundamental meaning resides in the kinds of felt relations they embody. Such a metaphysical vision makes processes and their interactions as real as seemingly permanent physical objects. In fact, the world of matter is seen to be a maelstrom of relations that balances itself through levels of polar oppositions. This is why, to repeat, a situation is the most really real dimension of the actual world. Every situation is made up of the ways in which its aspects, perspectives, and dimensions relate to each other. These relations can be concretely felt if the individual is attuned to their presence. Thus meaning itself is grounded in the felt relations that constitute the emergence of real novelty. The relations that make up the world of experience are therefore the matter to be attended to if satisfactory interactions with nature are to be had.

The term "associated life" is an important consolidation of Dewey's metaphysics, aesthetics, and social philosophy. It is not possible in Dewey's view to live a solitary existence. By nature and by circumstance we are not built to live alone. We are through and through relational beings. Our experience generates feelings that concretely testify to their worth. We crave permanence but face continually changing conditions. Our feelings waver uncertainly between the precarious and the stable. What is needed is a way of living that balances permanence and change. Adjustments are needed even as achieved values are justly celebrated. Human beings move continually between the poles of belonging and not belonging. Our feelings tell us the quality of our relations. We are either in phase or out of phase. When we feel that we belong in a situation, then our associations are in gear; when the opposite occurs, our associated life falters: "To learn to be human is to develop through the give-and-take of communication an effective sense of being an individually distinctive member of a community; one who understands and appreciates its beliefs, desires and methods, and who contributes to a further conversion of organic powers into human resources and values. . . . [What is required] is the perfecting of the means and ways of communication of meanings so that genuinely shared interest in the consequences of interdependent activities may inform desire and effort and thereby direct action."[4]

Associated life encompasses all the major cultural interests discussed earlier. One cannot pursue aesthetic experience alone. It depends fully upon a community of perceivers and its traditions of interpretation. Induction into this community is one of the primary tasks of education. Similarly, religious experience is not confined to the solitary worship of an absolute. Authentic religious experience binds human beings together into a community loyal to an ideal that transcends the particularities of place, time, and circumstance. Ethics demands that we move beyond narrow personal concerns and take up a perspective that makes the interests of our fellow humans an essential part of our own happiness. Science is inherently an associated endeavor for its discoveries depend on the research of many collaborators. The necessity of associated work is even more true in the sphere of technological research and application. Finally, philosophy as the art of criticism is equally dependent upon the labors of many allies if it is to carry out its office. How else can the critique of values be carried out if it does not begin with the recognition of values already achieved by the community through its varied interests and aims?

A truly rich associated life demands the real presence of active and effective forms of communication. Meaning needs to be expressed and shared. No real difference ever grows out of vain attempts to make the world mirror our self-interest. Taken by itself, sheer expression never achieves anything valuable. *It must be able to be shared if it is to make a difference in the experience of the community.* This does not mean that art must level itself to the lowest common denominator and become a third-rate version of experience. It does, however, require that art in some form or other make its sense of wholeness available to be felt by others. And this remains true even if this requires enduring a long and difficult apprenticeship in new forms of perception. Art that remains idiosyncratic and the preserve of the elite contradicts itself. Its attempt to be special cancels out the very wholeness it is meant to celebrate. What cannot be offered to others cannot be shared. What cannot be shared has no meaning. What has no meaning makes no difference. What makes no difference is not real. Thus we are brought to the very gates of nihilism.

The deepest human need is for the experience of meaning. Humans must inhabit a world that is charged with meaning and that unveils further meaning as we participate in its processes. Without such a potential field of action, real human growth and development is not possible. Art is a major means for making such a world available for human beings. But it must be the kind of art that has escaped from the museums and now exists in the homes and streets of neighborhoods. It must in other words be genuinely democratic, a kind of felt understanding that does not draw invidious and useless distinctions between so-called fine and practical art. If art separates humans from their everyday practices, it ceases to be art. When the forms and institutions of social life lose their sense of contact with the concrete life of citizens, then one can be sure that art has ceased to be an important factor in associated life. When the criticism of values becomes more and more abstract and busies itself with ever narrower topics, then art has ceased to influence philosophy. When the power to shape and form public policy rests in the hands of a few professionals, then the democratic ideal has lost the enlivening power of art. Its future now lies in the hands of a class least likely to foster a genuinely democratic sharing of power. Finally, when the production, transmission, and consumption of goods and services for a profit becomes the chief goal of life, then market capitalism has truly triumphed. Art has been annihilated as a real force in the lives of ordinary citizens. Only the rich can now afford art. All others must watch from a respectful distance. The experience of meaning has degenerated into a sterile vision of the bottom line.

If relations are as real as the things they connect, then surely that by itself ought to be a sufficient argument for the importance of art in generating regions of meaning and value. But there is still another service that art provides human culture. Civilization is not a piecemeal affair of assorted values that get lumped together through the force of accident and circumstance. Every civilization worthy of the name finds varied ways to express the sense of importance that underlies its cultural achievements. This is because growth in meaning cannot be scattered or piecemeal. It must find itself bound into some form of meaningful whole. And it is precisely here that aesthetic experience becomes a crucial source of structured growth. A sense of wholeness, actual or potential, has to influence the ways in which values are ordered within community life.

Now wholeness does not mean perfection, nor does it entail completion. Such confused thinking harks back to an old way of thinking that Dewey sought to defeat. That mode of thought derived from the Greeks and was made official by medieval theologians privileging the permanent over the changing. It insisted on the superiority of fixed ends and static modes of being. What changed showed weakness and therefore was not a form of goodness. The good was unchangeable, effortless, unaffected by circumstances and beyond appeal. Such a perspective has no room for experience and the developmental qualities that are part of its process. In fact such a point of view has nothing to do with process. At best, it regards process as a subsidiary means that can be dismissed after it has done its job. The doings and sufferings of real experience have nothing to do with reality. Now Dewey regards this attitude as fatal for the future of philosophy. It makes philosophers part of an elite class untouched by life's hard knocks and untouchable by the common people. They assume royal rank and become a priesthood separated from the struggles of everyday experience. *No more separations.* Dewey insists that philosophy take its place alongside the other experiential disciplines: art, religion, ethics, science, and technology. This is why the concept of wholeness takes on a radically new meaning in Dewey's thought. It is the dynamic character of becoming rather than the static perfection of being that is the defining quality of the world of experience. What must be felt, understood, and managed is how events come to be through the intensity of their relations.

Dewey understood this transition from a world of fixed ideals and permanent substances to one characterized by change, action, and impermanence to be the foremost challenge facing the human race in the twentieth century:

> This change of human disposition toward the world does not mean that man ceases to have ideals, or ceases to be primarily a creature of the imagination. But it does signify a radical change in the character and function of the ideal realm man shapes for himself. In the classic philosophy, the ideal world is essentially a haven in which man finds rest from the storms of life; it is an asylum in which he takes refuge from the troubles of existence with the calm assurance that it alone is supremely real. When the belief that knowledge is active and operative takes hold of men, the ideal realm is no longer something aloof and separate; it is rather that collection of imagined possibilities that stimulates men to new efforts and realizations. It still remains true that the troubles which men undergo are the forces that lead them to project pictures of a better state of things. But the picture of the better is shaped so that it may become an instrumentality of action, while in the classic view the Idea belongs ready-made in a noumenal world. Hence it is only an object of personal aspiration or consolation, while to the modern, an idea is a suggestion of something to be done or of a way of doing.[5]

Wholeness in a world of experience exhibits four traits, each of which expresses the importance of process over permanence. These traits are unity, continuity, carryover, and communication. Unity functions within the quality of wholeness as a connecting bond that ties together the many differences involved in the process of experience. It does this by respecting the uniqueness of each part for its ability to contribute to the whole. It does not seek to eliminate discord. Rather it creates a wholeness out of the experience of difference. Wholeness comes about by reason of the creation of a contrast between the difference of the parts and the identity of the whole. All contrast is the bringing together of differences within a framework of identity. Such a unifying action leads to extraordinary intensity. By situating identity under difference, wholeness is experienced as a unity that does two things at the same time. First, it elicits a background of immensely important but dimly felt values. Second, it allows the particular concrete values in the foreground of experience to express themselves through the support provided by the background. Wholeness experienced as unity lets novelty and tradition come together in a contrast that evokes the solid achievement of the past even as it celebrates the birth of a new creation of value.

The second trait of wholeness in a world of experience is continuity. Since fixed ends are not the issue in a process universe, the central question facing those who would understand the structures of the real concerns the interactions between events. What keeps events from falling apart? Why do certain types of experience succeed while others fail? The concept of wholeness understood as the experience of continuity answers these questions. Recall that even at the outset of aesthetic experience there was a felt quality of potential wholeness pervading the situation. Continuity emerges out of this inaugural feeling, for as the experience develops, the connections between its parts become tighter and finally grow into each other. What was divided now expresses itself as part of a greater unity. Seen separately, there appears to be no connection between an apple and its seeds. Seen through the eyes of continuity, not only are the seeds and the fruit connected but the apple blossoms are also part of the whole.

What continuity brings to the experience of wholeness is a sense of tolerance for the uniqueness of the parts. For without their special particularity, no developing whole could emerge. Continuity also teaches patience, for it tells us that difference is not necessarily a stopping point. Out of difference a continuous identity can emerge but that identity must be viewed as a developing one. What continuity brings to the concept of wholeness is an endorsement of time as a real feature of the actual world. If time is a real dimension of our experience, then static forms of perfection are not among its major features. In fact, such achievements are dubious ones for they do not embody the salient traits of experience: change, development, process, and interactive wholeness. The static sense of wholeness that cherishes completion and perfection settles for a second rate version of experience. It may satisfy for a while but it has no lasting nutritional value.

I term the third trait of wholeness "carryover" because it best expresses how wholeness achieves the transition between phases of a process.[6] What occurs when wholeness is experienced is the transmission of the achieved values of the past into the future by reason of the present moment. This is basically what Dewey meant by calling aesthetic experience consummatory. He certainly did not mean the entombment of a certain form of value in a hallowed sepulcher. No shrines to experience are needed, wanted, or even desirable. What is meant by the term "carryover" is the way in which value is moved around within a situation. It affects first this node of importance, then that one, and then perhaps finally spreads throughout the entire experience. Carryover is the sign of successful continuity, for it marks the ways in which the achievements of the past find new expression in the future.

What is experienced in the present moment when wholeness is felt as the carryover of value from the past to the future is a feeling of the worthiness of past effort and struggle. The pain felt in experience has not been in vain. There is a wholeness affecting each dimension of the evolving situation. This is the best and only form of perfection available in a universe whose process is its reality. The developing whole completes itself by passing on its achievements to another situation. There the energies stored up in the successes of the past may be used for further efforts to achieve a satisfying balance of forces. This carryover of value will determine the further meaning of whatever values have so far been achieved.

Communication, the last trait of wholeness, brings us back to the central theme of this discussion. I have insisted that for Dewey communication is the central act of any civilization. Also I have been at pains to show the connections between his ethics, aesthetics, and metaphysics. Here we find one last opportunity to link together his thoughts on value and culture. In so doing, a final summary of his philosophy can also be expressed. What I mean by the relation between wholeness and communication is the way in which each dimension of an experience lies open to its other parts. There is a transparency between the varying dimensions of an experience such that each flows evenly and in an uninterrupted manner into the other parts of its field of influence. One might call it "rhythmic flexibility" or more simply, "flow." But what matters more than the word used is the experience itself. What happens is that the parts of an experience communicate with each other so that individual values are experienced and shared. This experience of shared meaning is a deeply internal one. It is marked by feelings that express the way in which a situation is transformed by the presence of real difference in an experience. Each mode of difference is accepted and allowed to influence the developing growth of the situation. The example may be a mundane one but consider the golf swing. Supposedly there are eighty-three movements involved in this one action. Yet the swing takes place as a whole. What happens in a successful golf swing is that each different movement (from forward waggle to completed follow-through) communicates its value to the next movement which in turn uses that information to impart further meaning to its movement. Thus each part is open to each other part and uses that part's difference to enhance its own participation in the process. The good golf swing is a whole that communicates wholeness throughout each of its parts. The result of the swing shows the quality of the communication: hook, slice, or straight down the fairway.

Communication provides wholeness with a sense of gathering strength as the experience builds towards its consummation. In this way communication also underscores a culture's values as they express themselves throughout the history of a community. The energy needed to restore, revive, or recreate values in the midst of social turmoil can only come from open communication between members of a community. Associated life requires bonds of transparency between different parts of the institutions and structures in question. Lying, false representation, disguised motives—these are the actions that weaken and finally kill community. The gain in energy acquired by consolidating the different dimensions of a community makes an incalculable difference to the life of its members. Now there is a source of meaning to draw on in an emergency. There is also a set of standards to employ in conflicts over values. Finally, there now exists a group of fellow members willing to assist in the difficult task of fostering the growth and development of the community. Their willingness grows in exact proportion to the openness with which they are treated. To the degree that they are given the opportunity to feel the feelings of others, to that same degree will they become reliable members of the community as a whole.

Wholeness constituted by unity, continuity, carryover, and communication characterizes the form of the good in a process world. When an experience is marked by such traits, it exhibits the highest excellence available within human experience. When a culture sustains a continuous level of such excellence, it has formed a uniquely powerful structure of organized experience, one that endorses and actively supports art, ethics, religion, science, and technology. And in so arranging its resources, such a culture also promotes ways of feeling, thinking, and doing that concretely enliven the real experience of its members. The good life is not reserved solely for those who can afford it. The good life is everywhere present in everyday experience. The situations that make up the life of this kind of community do not cease to have their tensions, strains, and difficulties. Paradise only happened once and even then it was a myth. But the doings and undergoings felt throughout the community's experience are guided by a vision of further wholeness: a form of unity, continuity, carryover, and communication that invites each member to hold together for the sake of a whole greater than the sum of its parts. The communication of such a whole is the major task of a community's cultural life.

Working Connections with Confucius: He, Xin, Xin*, Junzi

There have been a number of working connections already established between the thought of John Dewey and that of Confucius. The first chapter discussed *dao*, *de*, and *ren* as measures and means whereby human beings experience satisfaction in their lives. The previous chapter's discussion of felt intelligence provided three more connections, *zhi*, *yi*, and *li*. They showed the ways in which Dewey and Confucius ground their understanding of life's struggles in the aesthetic order where feelings of intensity, integrity, width, and depth guide the way toward growth.

This chapter concludes by looking at four more Confucian concepts: *he*, *xin* , *xin**, and *junzi*. These concepts find their full meaning in lived cultural experience. Confucius has a term for this: *he*. It means "harmony" and it is not to be equated with nice things and sweet melodies. Harmony is the way in which authoritative human beings bring difference into their experience as a productive quality:

> Master You said: "Achieving harmony (*he*) is the most valuable function of observing ritual propriety (*li*). In the way of the Former Kings, this achievement of harmony made them elegant, and was a guiding standard in all things large and small. But when things are not going well, to realize harmony just for its own sake without regulating the situation through observing ritual propriety will not work."[7]

To gain a full sense of its meaning it is necessary to introduce two more terms from Confucius's philosophy: *xin* and *xin** The first term, *xin*, is used by the Chinese to identify the source of thinking and feeling that lies at the core of human life. It is best translated as "heart-mind." It expresses in one word what Dewey sought all his life to achieve: *the reconciliation of the body and the mind.* *Xin** is key to the arts of communication that are so important for Dewey's philosophy. It is brilliantly translated by Hall and Ames as "living up to one's word."[8] Harmony is achieved when the heart (which is the source of feeling) and the mind (which is the source of thinking) know the same thing— and when that experiential meaning is expressed in human personal and social action:

> Master *You* said: "That making good on one's word (*xin**) gets one closer to being appropriate (*yi*) is because then what one says will bear repeating. This being deferential gets one close to observing ritual propriety (*li*) because it keeps disgrace and insult at a distance. Those who are accommodating and do not lose those with whom they are close are deserving of esteem."[9]

Harmony closes the circle on the interrelated themes of this chapter. It unites thought and feeling, inquiry and art, and human growth and social development.

Culture is the effort to stabilize experience through the creation and maintenance of forms of wholeness. Philosophy is the critic of the values upheld by civilizations. Culture and philosophy come together when the three forms (feeling, willing, and doing) that make up felt intelligence are called into play and effectively strengthen the webs of experience that feed and support human beings. Without culture these ties that bind human beings and their environments dry up and wither. Dessicated experience is no experience at all.

Feeling is what constitutes the core of human growth and social development. It finds its connection with Confucius through the idea of the heartmind, or *xin*:

> The Master said, "With my disciple, *Yan Hui*, he could go for several months without departing from authoritative (*ren*) thoughts and feelings; as for the others, only every once in a long while, might authoritative thoughts and feelings make an appearance.[10]

Feeling and thought are already together in Chinese experience. This comes from centuries of practicing the rituals that govern civilized relations. *Li* is the summation of this interactive process. When the culture's public body (or "shadow soma" or "habitual body") becomes rooted in the habits of a community, a bond of feeling weaves its members together into depths of understanding. Symbols are felt through the heartmind of the people. If these gestures towards wholeness become automatic and empty, the people sense this and turn their backs on the political and cultural institutions that are supposed to help them grow. Cynicism and apathy take the place of organic participation. Transparency is lost. Practice in the arts of deceit then becomes a major cultural occupation. Rich, robust harmony is lost. Its noncoercive drawing power (*de*) fades and is replaced by violent political action:

> Ji Kangzi asked Confucius about governing effectively, saying, "What if I kill those who have abandoned the way (*dao*) to attract those who are on it?"
>
> "If you govern effectively," Confucius replied, "what need is there for killing? If you want to be truly adept, the people will also be adept. The excellence (*de*) of the exemplary person (*junzi*) is the wind, while that of the petty person is the grass. As the wind blows, the grass is sure to bend."[11]

It is the same with *thinking*. Inquiry becomes the employment of "experts" whose conclusions somehow miraculously affirm the wishes of those in power. Instead of being a pathway to improvement, inquiry moves the community further and further away from participatory experience. Soul-killing abstractions dominate discourse and the helpless and the needy are buried in a tomb of statistics. The continuity between means and ends is broken and such monstrosities as the low-income housing project loom up in the slums of cities. Even the words "low-income," "housing" and "project" betray the underlying lack of heart in such social endeavors. Where inquiry was supposed to let us realize the good, it is now used to numb us to the bleakness caused by social despair. Situations are particular and inquiry's first task is to recognize that characteristic. Science by its nature seeks the statistically normative. It cannot reach the realm of quality and value without the assistance of the aesthetic. Instrumental and consummatory experience are inextricably bound together. Confucius recognized this first. "The Master said, 'Exemplary persons seek harmony not sameness; petty persons, then, are the opposite."[12] John Dewey, the "Second Confucius," also saw the necessity of bringing things together productively.

Doing as a cultural practice is not to be identified with fixing problems. It is directly concerned with the cultural task of deepening the patterns of meaning that constitute communal existence. To do is to "live up to one's word (*xin**)" in such a way as to make real the values implied in the community's self-understanding. If experience means to live, and inquiry means to live better, then to live up to one's word is the vital act that grounds personal and social existence. Without it, we are fools to believe what we are told. Transparency is the virtue that a true *dao* grants. It is what Confucius demands over and over again in the *Analects*. But it is not a monochrome, mechanical honesty. It is an honesty geared to particular situations. One is not obliged to give the full story to the four-year-old who asks about the nature of certain sexual acts. The child cannot handle that information. Similarly, social discourse must be tailored to the situation at hand. There is a time for protest and a time for courtesy. Doing involves knowing the appropriate fit between the act taken and the situation for which it is intended.

Symbolic decay is the worst fate that can befall a community. Instead of calling forth depth of participation, our symbols evoke contempt. Rather than inviting thoughtful response, our symbols make a mockery of what is intended. The hypocrisy behind them is seen for what it really is: failure to live up to one's word. Communication is shattered. This was the state of things when Confucius began to teach:

"The Master said, 'The ancients were loath to speak because they would be ashamed if they personally did not live up to what they said.'"[13]

A similar situation faced Dewey. Harmony (*he*) seemed quite impossible. Whether it was the never-ending violence marking the period of the Warring States or war between capital and labor, both thinkers faced a similar challenge. Both managed to become authoritative persons within the maelstrom of their cultures. Both saw the essence of their task to be the reconstruction of the lines of communication spanning individuals and their society. Both agreed on the general traits of reality. They saw it as processive, changing, and in need of wise intervention. Both agreed that the social order was the primary element in this task of reconstruction. Both were way seekers relying on experience to bring about their desired goals. And what about us? Is there a way to use experience to improve our world and defuse its crises?

When the social tools of feeling, willing, and doing become settled habits, then exemplary people (*junzi*) take their place in the social order. Such people are priceless centers of concern and creativity within the community. The fundamental contribution that *junzi* make to a community is a power to communicate at a unified level of felt intelligence. Feeling, willing, and doing are made existentially one. Their persons and characters shine through their actions. Transparency and a clear character inform their habitual presence in the community. They can be counted on to bring appropriate normative measures to bear even in the most difficult of situations. In fact they transform situations by reason of their personal integrity:

> The Master remarked that Zichan accorded with the way (*dao*) of the exemplary person (*junzi*) in four respects: he was gracious in deporting himself, he was deferential in serving his superiors, he was generous in attending to needs of the common people, and he was appropriate (*yi*) in employing their services.[14]

Exemplary persons show the way to others. Their conduct is their speech and their choice of actions seizes the imagination of the community. In social life we learn more quickly by witnessing the behavior of others than by intellectualizing about the best way to achieve good results:

> The Master said, "Exemplary persons (*junzi*) learn broadly of culture, discipline this learning through observing ritual propriety (*li*), and moreover, in so doing, can remain on course without straying from it.[15]

What is most characteristic of this kind of person is a certain broadness of temperament that is ready to harmonize with what is met on the road of life. Where the *junzi* is big, others are small; the exemplary person (*junzi*) is calm and unperturbed; the petty person is always agitated and anxious.

Ames and Rosemont summarize the active presence of the *junzi* with these words:

> [T]he junzi is almost always described (for the benefit of the disciples), not instructed (because presumably he does not need it). He has traveled a goodly distance along the way, and lives a goodly number of roles. A benefactor to many, he is still a beneficiary of others like himself. While he is still capable of anger in the presence of inappropriateness and concomitant injustice, he is in his person tranquil. He knows many rituals and much music, and performs all of his functions not only with skill, but with grace, dignity, and beauty, and he takes delight in the performances. He is still filial toward his parents and elders, but now takes "all under *tian*" [heaven] as his dwelling. While real enough to be still capable of the occasional lapse in his otherwise exemplary conduct . . . he is resolutely proper in the conduct of his roles—conduct which is not forced, but rather effortless, spontaneous, creative. There is, in sum, a very strong aesthetic and ethical dimension to his life; he has reauthorized the *li*, and is therefore a respected author of the dao of humankind.[16]

Human culture needs such an individual. The whole thrust of the Confucian vision is to bridge the separation between the social order and the aims of the individual. The parallels with Dewey should by now be obvious. It remains to summarize his qualifications to be called a "Second Confucius."

"A Second Confucius"

Our civilization is characterized by a devout belief in science as the most reliable way to discover truth. This belief is wedded to a commitment to technology as the way to make good on the findings of science. This has led to extraordinary advances in biogenetics, the neurosciences, medicine, space exploration, and new forms of communications. The same belief has also led to the possession of the means to destroy civilization as well as staggering environmental problems. More recently, an intense drive to create free market capitalism run by multinational corporations has taken over global politics and spawned a massive split between the very rich and the very poor. These developments are sufficient to destroy the many ways in which particular cultures have established and maintained their ways of life. Tied together they are a cultural tsunami threatening the forms of value so far realized by the human race.

Our time is much different than that of Dewey and even more remote from the age of Confucius. How does one forge a genuine *dao* that respects and extends the traditions of these two great philosophers? And can a corresponding philosophy stand against the destructive forces inherent in our present world situation. Such a task is the problem faced by comparative philosophy. As a discipline this branch of philosophy is quite young. Included among its contemporary practitioners are Roger Ames and the late David Hall as well as those philosophers involved in what has recently been called Boston Confucianism.[1] Still in an embryonic form, the discipline continues to test out various approaches and methodologies. It is, I believe, too early to set out a formal definition of comparative philosophy. But Alfred North Whitehead has a very valuable suggestion as to how to approach this task: "*The first chapter* in philosophic approach should consist in a free examination of some ultimate notions as they occur naturally in daily life."[2]

From the perspective of this study Whitehead's suggestion comes down to undertaking a free examination of the following ultimate notions: experience, inquiry, and community life. Each concept has its Confucian connection. For experience we have the concept of *dao*. For inquiry, there is the concept of *li*. Community life is represented by the Confucian idea of *ren*. These ultimate notions are a set of tools for dealing with the problems caused by globalization.

Dao and Experience

It is best to begin with experience, which displays four characteristics. It is *aesthetic, interpretive, engaged, and corrective.*[3] If experience is a *dao*, then there are many modes of behaving on a way. To name a few, one can find a way, seek a way, walk on a way, or even lose one's way. I suggest that the primordial mode of experiencing a way is to feel it. Feeling one's way indicates the intimate connection between the way and the way walker. Feeling is the translation of the Greek word *aisthesis*, which is the root of the English "aesthetics." To call experience aesthetic is to draw attention to its most rudimentary lived level. One quite literally feels one's way along and uses all one's senses in the process. But central to feeling is touch. We use our fingers and toes, and all the dimensions of our body to feel our way along. It is this basic act of feeling one's way that brings together the American and Chinese understanding of *dao* and experience. The act is not primarily cognitive but still conveys vitally important information. We have succeeded so far but we still have a way to go. There were rough spots but also smooth ones. Sometimes we had to become like children and squeeze through various cracks and fissures. As a *dao*, experience demands trust, risk, cooperation, and participation.

By uncovering and articulating the root meaning of experience as the act of feeling one's way through a situation, Dewey is able to provide human beings with a way around the splits preventing wholeness of experience. To feel one's way is to simultaneously encounter both instrumental and consummatory experience. It is a method with an end in view. It gives knowledge but is not rooted entirely in the cognitive. Its most basic sources flow from the human body as it participates in the problems to be solved.

To feel one's way is to become once again that "live creature" of which Dewey so eloquently spoke:

> To grasp the sources of aesthetic experience, it is, therefore, necessary to have recourse to animal life below the human scale. The activities of the fox, the dog, and the thrush may at least stand as reminders and symbols of that unity of experience which we so fractionize when work is labor, and thought withdraws us from the world. The live animal is fully present, all there, in all of its actions: in its wary glances, its sharp sniffings, its abrupt cocking of ears. All senses are equally on the *qui vive*. As you watch, you see motion merging into sense and sense into motion—constituting that animal grace so hard for man to rival. What the live animal retains from the past and what it expects from the future operate as directions in the present. The dog is never pedantic nor academic; for these things arise only when the past is severed in consciousness from the present and is set up as a model or a storehouse upon which to draw. The past absorbed into the present carries on; it presses forward.[4]

To feel one's way is to stalk the goodness that hides in the depths of our problems. That goodness is the unification of the divisions—personal, social, and cultural—that starve us of wholeness. There is a strange quality to this form of goodness that heals the human spirit. Let us go back to the act of feeling our way and try to remember those times when we carried out such risky adventures. Is it not instructive that it is often childhood experiences that are most vividly recalled? Somehow we had to really feel our way without the help of previous experience. Now I ask, what got us through those times? I believe it was the way in which we could open ourselves to what was going on all around us. Panic forces us to close off our bodies. When we successfully felt our way through a tight situation, it was because we emptied ourselves of everything but the experience itself. We became what we were doing. The split between being and doing dissolved and our wholeness with the situation saw us through.

I want to highlight two important aspects of this act of feeling one's way:

- First, our analysis tells us that there is something about emptiness and goodness that connects them on a primordial level.

- Second, if we are to experience some of this kind of goodness in our lives, we, too, have to empty ourselves so that the feeling of a situation can be felt, lived, and passed through.

This act of removing our past prejudices is fundamental to truthful interpretation. To interpret is to underscore what has been achieved in the carryover of the past into the present. Stuck in the past, no novelty can emerge. Marooned in the present, no sense of comparative value can emerge. Both dispositions threaten the quality of future judgments. To feel one's way is to *interpret*. To feel one's way *engages* the whole person—body, mind, and spirit—in the most intense activity. To feel one's way is to *correct* one's way of proceeding even as one advances further along the way. None of these vital actions can take place unless we are engaged with the situation and bring to it the full measure of our human powers.

Correction and *engagement* are the final features of experience. They are the way signs Dewey uses to feel his way through the fissures, gaps, and spaces that open up into new dimensions of experience. What makes Dewey a double of Confucius is this patient attention to the particulars of experience—an attitude of caring and watchfulness that marks all great aesthetic achievement. Correction signifies our responsibility to put right what has gone astray. In Confucian terms to correct is to rectify a situation by adjusting the misshapen dimensions that plague its balance and stability. To correct is to address the doings and undergoings of experience so as to bring forth consummatory qualities previously absent. But such correction is also instrumental in the sense that many ways may have to be tried out before the most suitable one is found. The act of correction is experimental. No fixed ends should hem it in. To decide beforehand what the outcome should be is to fail to engage the situation in an open, tolerant way. Interpretation and correction are the ways and means whereby genuine engagement is felt. To feel one's way along the narrow edge of a problem without resorting to easy fixes is to show courage in the face of the problematic and hope in the face of potential failure. It is to be fully engaged in the experience undergone.

All four aspects of the *dao* of experience—feeling, interpretation, correction, and engagement—demand the exercise of the virtues of faith and hope. Both virtues find their concrete expression in acts of trust. To trust despite previous failure is to commit one's humanity to the good. Effective action within the aesthetic domain requires a trust in the power of beauty—a quality rarely thought to be a source of strength. Similarly, interpretation and correction demand conviction that openness and a willingness to struggle with difficulties can ultimately make great differences in human life. All this is to repeat the fact that experience is the ultimate transformative agent. To alter circumstances, to shift environmental conditions, to reshape one's attitude toward others—these are engaged acts of transformation that can bring about cultural reconciliation.

A major reason why Dewey is a "Second Confucius" is that he, like the Master, saw experience as the forge within which personal and social change could be welded anew. Change is not easy. Transition to better states of being is a unique cultural event. It takes risk, trust, faith, hope, and wise planning. Traditions wisely understood and creatively used are the background against which such reconstruction can be successfully undertaken. Confucius was the sage who saw the necessity of carrying this out on a wide social scale. Dewey envisaged a similar reform effort more than twenty-five hundred years later. Whatever differences separate both philosophers, one concept unites them both. It is the fact that the way of transformation is grounded in experience of all kinds. It is the person who shapes the way and not the way that shapes the person. Experience is the living tissue of the *dao*.

Li and Inquiry

There is another dimension that welds together the thoughts of Confucius and Dewey. It is the hard-won concept of inquiry as an affair of both the heart and the mind. I have already spoken of the act of felt intelligence as the core of their method of repairing the errors and mistakes of the social order. What must be erased from the Confucian reputation is the suspicion that a mandarin smugness infects its rituals. This is the result of misunderstanding the reasons behind the Confucian passion for attention to details. Particulars are the root and branch of the aesthetic sense of order that lies at the base of *li* understood as "observing ritual propriety."[5] It is both the unique particularity of the social order's panoply of gestures as well as how these gestures relate to particular situations that is at the heart of the Confucian concept of *li*. How we treat others experientially in important moments is the outcome of the rites we use to address, help, and support them. These must be done with a full heart and an awakened mind; otherwise, they fall empty and do not allow us genuine participation in the experience of others.

How can we help with social problems unless we admit that they are there? This was Dewey's question. He backed it up with another question: How can we know their problems unless we can feel the situations in which others find themselves? His response involved the development of a concrete process of inquiry. Situations are to be turned into problems felt as out of place, broken rhythms in the texture of social experience. These disruptions affected us all. Everything depended upon finding a way to communicate the feelings of sorrow and discontent that rooted themselves in these problems: slums, education, labor, poverty, life rendered unsettled and precarious.

As discussed previously, *li* is to be understood in connection with the concepts of *yi* and *zhi* where *yi* denotes hitting the mark or bringing correctness into the sphere of real relations and *zhi* denotes the act of realizing the right solution for particular problems. When wound together into an authentic personal gesture, these meanings signal the presence of a *junzi,* the master of communication. What this social artist brings to expression are ways to change disunity into wholeness and separations into healed experiences. For it is the purpose of *li* as a cultural resource to mend the breaches in public order whether they be brought about by personal loss, social injustice, or natural disasters. It is to the rightly timed gesture that the *junzi* looks and it is the unity expressed in these acts that the community feels.

Social feeling depends on the active presence of a shadow soma, that vague but deeply felt sense of corporeal identification required to bring split souls together. Any smugness or artificiality is quickly sensed by the public and that is why *li* must always be flexible and attuned to the situation at hand. Dewey's work has often been associated with a mindless trust in the idea of progress. Such blind confidence is not at the heart of his thought and practice.[6] Given, however, his stress on instrumentalism it is easy to see how such distortions could be read into his philosophy. It is therefore all the more important to restate his basic idea of amelioration. Dewey sought to better the situation, not perfect it. A deeper comprehension of this drive toward the better can be had through the Chinese doctrine of change as the alteration of situations from one extreme to another. What underlies this understanding is the doctrine of the correlativity of all states of being. It is, of course, best known in the West as the complementary unity underlying correlative states of yin and yang. It is the functional equivalent of what chapter 2 called "felt intelligence."

What is needed to tone down suspicions about Dewey's trust in an inevitable movement toward progress is a commitment to a far more realistic idea of causal efficacy. By this I mean that the doctrine of yin and yang implies an ameliorative sensibility much better attuned to realistic understandings of the possibilities of social change. What is to be looked for is not some utopian transformation of unsettled conditions but rather sets of gradual returns to states of equilibrium. These recoveries are made possible by finding the right purchase in different situations. It is by initiating new pivots of influence that situations can get turned around. The goal is wholeness and unity, not radical transformations.

An effective *li* drives human attention toward what is possible for the concrete world of value in which we live. This actual world spins on a delicate axis that balances out unsettled situations and thereby turns them into problems to be solved. This could not be done if *li* were merely the art of hoodwinking the public by means of hypocritical forms of ritualized concern. As the history of China shows, mandarin smugness hiding hierarchical agendas is quickly uncovered. In the present day we have the scandals of theft found at the heart of free market capitalism. It is the well-formed heartmind that detects the phoniness behind gestures of social reform that go nowhere. The most effective instrument in the ameliorist's toolbox turns out to be this hard-won sense of what is possible and what is impossible in given situations. It is "the wisdom to know the difference" that makes the difference in matters of social concern.

The art of gaining power over circumstances was one of Dewey's major goals. Power comes in many forms and shapes. It cuts both ways and can be as dangerous to its owner as it can be to its victim. A careful sense of balance is needed to replace the worse with the better. The flash of insight, the apt gesture, the right moment seized, the plan accomplished come as much from a sense of timing as from the power amassed to carry out the project. Hall and Ames have rightly termed it the "contextualizing art."[7] Recall Zhuangzi's butcher, whose cleaver remains newly sharpened in the face of nineteen years of use. The degree of deftness used in social action determines the quality of its outcome. To practice felt intelligence requires years of disciplined learning. I believe that is why Confucius declared his only task to be that of a learner. The art of learning is the art of finding one's spot and keeping a balance throughout the pushes and pulls of experience as it tugs us now here, now there throughout the personal and the public sphere:

> The Master said, "Deference unmediated by observing ritual propriety (*li*) is lethargy; caution unmediated by observing ritual propriety is timidity; boldness unmediated by ritual propriety is rowdiness; candor unmediated by observing ritual propriety is rudeness. Where exemplary persons (*junzi*) are earnestly committed to their parents, the people will aspire to authoritative conduct (*ren*); where they do not neglect their old friends, the people will not be indifferent to each other.[8]

Dewey's insistence on the primacy of the aesthetic suggests that he, too, knew the importance of this art. To inquire into the human world in order to make it better demands much more than statistical analysis. It needs more than the application of more funds. It requires something more than new institutions and power structures. That "something more" is achieved by the full participation of the human person in the arts of life.

Li aims at what is relevantly excellent. It seeks to make real the good that lurks hidden in the circumstances of life's problems. It demands a unification of feeling, thinking, and doing within the human person. Without such integration little can be accomplished by way of reconstructing experiences that are felt as off center, unjust, cruel, and false to real human goodness. Thus, *zhi* and *yi* become part of the "centripetal harmony"[9] caused by the presence of an effective *li*. The shadow soma brought about by good ritual draws into its circle of influence the scattered and shattered domains of lost social values. It can heal broken hearts and shambled minds because it invites participation in new forms of unity and wholeness. This is not the work of a moment, a single day, or even sometimes a single lifetime. We are talking about the creation of a "habitual body." It is a work that enables an "Us" to emerge from the rubble of circumstance and injustice. This "We" is Confucian insofar as it seeks to realize the good and authorize it in real acts of social justice. It is Deweyan in the sense that it invokes the priority of the social over the selfish and finds ways and means to celebrate the new forms of association that have emerged from the ruins of past losses. This is amelioration at its best. It aims at creating new forms of meaning to be shared by those committed to community as a good prior to all forms of individual liberty.

When these new communities take shape, their ways of appreciating life will run more along qualitative lines than quantitative measures. The *intensity* of experience will matter more than personal gain. The *integrity* of experience will stand as more important than individual moments of pleasure. The *wholeness* of experience will draw more participants into its ambit than the lure of distracting sideshows. Finally, the *depth* of experience will guarantee that more value lies ahead if the community commits itself to a shared future rich in the rituals of associated life. These are the same norms used earlier to measure the authentic meaning of inquiry carried out in the spirit of *li*. It bridges the gap between the personal dimension and the social environment. Both regions of experience demand rituals of effective inquiry.

Ren and Communal Culture

I ended the last section with a brief listing of the four norms relevant to healthy community life. They also define what Confucius means by *ren*, the ultimate goal of human existence. To be *ren* means to have become human. Ames translates it as becoming an "authoritative person,"[10] by which he intends a series of meanings. Authoritative people create their own spaces within the circumstances of their time. This activity is attuned to the situation and at the same time moves it in a more unified direction. The resources used in such an effort spring from the social traditions of their culture. What makes them *ren* is the creative twist put on this effort such that new connections with the real are laid down. This novel track lets human energies play more freely and more effectively within the situation. One result is that the qualitative presence of *ren* authors a more humane tone within the sphere of human action. What *ren* authenticates is the qualitative difference made by humans when they act in an excellent manner. Humans broaden the way so that what is better can emerge from what is worse. Released from the constrictions of the past, the authoritative person brings into play fresh energies with which to deal with the precarious and unsettled dimensions of experience.

But none of this can happen unless there is a fund of symbols through which the significance of these new actions can be communicated to others. Culture depends on the vitality of such communicative codes. The more daring the authoritative action, the more resonant must be the communicative resources of the culture. Great deeds require great signs and vice versa. That is why Confucius spent so much time on the "Odes" and the "Rectification of Names." Without a symbolic code that can be revised during times of crisis, what Dewey calls "associated life" has little or no hope of survival in times of drift, decay, or upheaval. The authoritative person has recourse to these symbols and brings them forth in new clusters of meaning. Dewey provides two good examples of this important connection between *ren* and culture. First, there is his *Reconstruction in Philosophy* (1920), a work, interestingly enough, first tried out in Asia. In this rethinking of the foundations of Western thought and culture, he takes on certain basic cultural assumptions and gives them new meanings. For example, the whole idea of matter as vacuous actuality is jettisoned along with the anti-idealism that it spawned. In its place he offers a dynamic concept of the world as housing in its material resources energies for significant change. Further, he then yokes this reconstructed idea of the material world to Darwin's concept of adaptation. The result is a new vision for philosophy's future. It is to assist in the criticism of abstractions that hold back the betterment of humankind. All the old familiar ideas of philosophers—causality, means and ends, value, transcendence, and immanence—take on new meaning. Dewey has offered a new authoritative account of some of the most important building blocks of Western culture.

Ren enters the world of the public thinker with recharged clarity and force. The philosopher is given a new office. The role of the "public intellectual" takes shape before our eyes. This new responsibility is carried to another level when Dewey publishes his *Individualism Old and New* (1929). Here in the midst of the Great Depression, Dewey seeks to summon new life for the idea of the relation between government and the individual. By recasting the concept of associated life he is able to address such significant human issues as "The Lost Individual" and "Capitalistic or Public Socialism." In both instances he provides a new understanding of human welfare as dependent upon shared meanings rather than material wealth. Person-in-Community becomes a genuine theme for philosophic reflection. Once again, *ren* increases by reason of the philosopher's ability to imbue old ideas with fresh and important new life.

Both books signal a reconstruction of old forms of social behavior. In the case of *Reconstruction in Philosophy*, the relation between the spiritual and the material world is turned upside down. What was once scorned as merely inert "stuff" is now seen to harbor the values of the future. Old loyalties and affiliations give way to new ways of understanding the place of the human in the material world. *Ren* takes on much deeper significance as humans become responsible not only for their ethical ideals but also for the material means of realizing them. Suddenly, the entire environmental background of our culture looms into view as a matter of deep human concern. Ecology emerges as a fundamental discipline needed for the reconstruction of our cultural standards.

Similarly, *Individualism Old and New* places a new demand on an America grown accustomed to celebrating rites of individualized freedoms. Stiffened versions of freedom are challenged by more flexible normative measures. The fact that we are our brother's keeper is argued in the most forceful way. Old institutional arrangements are challenged and critiqued for their inability to share power with the unfortunate. *Ren* enters precisely at those interstices of the social order where human needs are most likely to be neglected. Associated life is declared a field for innovation and reform. What looms forth is a stunning array of opportunities for human growth and development geared to social participation rather than isolated individual action. Communication across social classes is now a necessity rather than an infrequent and haphazard matter. How one sees America is now a cultural question of the utmost importance.

The answers to the problem of the human communication of values that Dewey provided earlier in an analysis entitled *The Public and Its Problems* (1927) now take on a new urgency. Democracy itself is what is being discussed and crucial for its future is the concept of the "Great Community." Is it possible to bring together such diverse energies and goals? What are the resources to carry out such a task? Dewey recognizes the limits of inquiry in the social sciences. The book ends with an appeal to the necessity of local community life.

How does the local blend with the global? Is it even possible? An adequate answer to these questions involves two dimensions. First, it must be determined what it means to be human. This is the question of *ren* recast for the twenty-first century. Second, the arts of communication must be reexamined to locate the source of distributing clearly and equitably the meanings of the new individualism and its relation to social action. As Dewey says, "Presentation is fundamentally important, and presentation is a question of art."[11] And so we come full circle back to Confucius and the importance of the arts of communication. Be it through ritual forms, cultural gestures, evocative prose, poetic utterance, movies, music, media, or any of the arts, what is at stake is the future of *ren*. Social life and individual satisfaction fade into each other when effective communication takes place.

This brings us to what makes all this possible: the act of sharing. Dewey calls it a mystery and Confucius expresses wonder that it happens at all. One thing is for sure: the act of sharing means that there is more than one person in the neighborhood. Central to the idea of sharing is the capacity to participate. Sharing and participation are ancient philosophic themes. They are at the heart of both Eastern and Western philosophy. I suggest we take cues from both cultural resources. From the East, I borrow the idea of yin and yang and from the West I take the idea of the relation between structure and value. Yin and yang are complementary structures that express in different ways different arrangements of the expression of value. Yin and yang exist as part of an arrangement of complementary qualities within particular events. The degree to which something is yang is correlative to the situation in which it is located. Westerners, especially Americans, are prone to sexualize the terms so that yang is masculine and yin is feminine. Rather, yang means the sunny side of the hill; yin, the shady part. Thus depending upon the time of day or even the weather, one side can be more or less yin and more or less yang. The qualities are therefore correlative to each other and draw meaning from the relation between them rather than their own essences. Grasping and understanding relational correlates is the way to Confucian wisdom. Over and over again, he counsels his students to be wary of the situation and the way in which its various domains play out. As Roger Ames puts it, the task of making the right choice depends upon "a mapping out and an unraveling of the phenomenon's multiple correlations and of the relationships and conditions that make up its context."[12]

I have elsewhere called this way of judging situations "normative thinking."[13] It relies on the norms used to establish the relations between the parts of complex situations. For example, what one calls a good house depends upon the interrelations between many different values: location, price, size, age, and so on. Each of these values takes on a normative weight in terms of its importance in shaping our understanding of the value of the house in question. Normative thinking is therefore always appreciative thinking since it seeks the worth of what is being judged. It esteems rather than analyzes, prizes rather than defines. The correlation used to scale the value of a situation is set in terms of how it harmonizes components. These components can be understood as complex or simple depending upon the roles they play in making up the circumstances at play within the situation. Also each event has essential and conditional features that contribute in different ways to the complex to be judged. Granted, the word "essential" will alarm certain interpreters of the Chinese way of thinking; they ought to give it a chance since what is essential in one situation need not be essential in the same situation at another time. For example, gender may be irrelevant in one project and entirely essential in another. When it comes to pregnancy, it is essential; when it comes to employment it is not. In other words, a shifting essential is not the same as fixed Western essences. The interrelations between situations are to be viewed as moving toward the creation of different types of continuity.

The identification and creation of harmony is what is at stake in both Confucian and Deweyan thinking. A harmony is at one level a very simple matter. It is what it is and is no other. This is its simplicity. At the same time every harmony has a complex side since it must draw together differences so that a new unity becomes present. A harmony correlates simplicity and complexity such that a unique particular unity takes the place of previously splintered components. Identity is achieved through the right mixing of difference.

Harmony is the most powerful act of sharing through participation. The Chinese do it through correlative thinking. American naturalism leans on the relational power of form. Form here means the limit that defines a particular kind of event. Hatred is not love; orange is not blue; and a circle is not a square. It is the power of laying down a limit that is most important in the doctrine of form. The question of its eternal immutability is not to the point. Harmonic creativity is a matter of knowing the de facto limits inherent in events and situations and using them to broaden and deepen what can be shared. Forms participate in the facts and shape what they are. Without form there would be only the inscrutable defying all attempts at understanding. Form in a process world is through and through finite. In fact, value is the gift of finitude since it is the limitation set on situations that generates their coming to be.

Just how well does such normative thinking square with Confucian philosophy? A valid answer depends on the relation of four ideas: correlative thinking, limit, participation, and sharing. To correlate events means to have some measure by which the matters in question can be brought into a comparison. This measure for Confucius is twofold: a return to stability marked by moral excellence (*de*) and a reconstruction of the harmonies that guide the associated life of the people. Dewey regards ethics as the effort to promote progress towards growth. This norm in its turn is to be understood as the establishment of deeper, wider, and more stable social relations. In this sense the good is firmly grounded in social relations. Correlative thinking is hereby expanded beyond the search for metaphors that can tie together particulars. It becomes rather the effort to cast the widest possible net so as to promote good relations between humans. It is precisely at this point that the search for appropriate limits takes on a new meaning. There is much to be said for the Chinese sense of humanity as an essentially social achievement. But there is another side to experience that must be given its due: the personal dimension that is at the heart of genuine encounters with the other. When it comes to human social experience, it is persons that carry it forward. Meanings must reach deep down into the consciousness of individuals. Confucius aptly expresses the importance of finding this mean:

> Zigong inquired, "Who is of superior character, Zizhang or Zixia? The Master replied, "Zizhang oversteps the mark, and Zixia falls short of it."
> "Does this make Zizhang better?" asked Zigong.
> "One is as bad as the other," replied Confucius.[14]

Artists, in their uniqueness and particular genius, are the epitome of such personal contributions to social experience. Here is where Dewey's genius can expand the Confucian ideal of *ren*. The exceptional and the novel need not be regarded as a threat to social conformity. In fact, just the opposite is the case. For it is Dewey's contention that the artist lays down the pathway (or *dao*) by which saving alternatives sink into cultural consciousness. The limit of which I spoke earlier is not a barrier but a starting point from which new experiments in quality and goodness can take off. The exchange between artist and public on new forms of meaning is precisely what the community needs in order to test imaginatively the limits of what is considered appropriate. By varying perspective and shifting types of media, new attention can be drawn to alternative possibilities. By providing experimental limits for social consciousness the artist fulfills a primary social function. For an ameliorist like Dewey it is never a question of rejecting old ideas or brashly endorsing new ones. Space needs to be provided for trying out the new and esteeming its worth. Artists do this as part of their calling.

Participation and sharing are the last two ideas to be discussed as part of this analysis of a kind of normative thinking formed through the fusion of Confucian and American philosophy. Participation is irrevocably yoked to values and the norms by which they are measured. Robert Neville provides a set of theses by which the interplay between normative measure, value, and situations can be understood:

- *For any plurality of things there may be various ways in which they can be together, and the more elegant ways are the better ways.*

- *A mode of harmony or structure in which things are together is a normative measure—that is, a good way for the things to be together.*

- *A normative measure is the structure of a harmony according to which the particular constituents of the harmony are elegantly joined.*[15]

Now "elegant" here means that which does the most with the least effort. This quality has a direct bearing on the second topic of our discussion, sharing. For sharing must accord due space to all dimensions of the situation under consideration. Elegance is therefore a primary condition for good forms of openness whereby diversity is granted a place in a rich unity. It is the economy of elegance that needs to be noticed. Less is more in both the Confucian and the Deweyan vision of the good.

What needs to be shared is the meaning that will bring into harmony the unsettled or precarious relations existing within problematic situations. Such a meaning ought to arise from the traditions that support cultures. For Confucius it may very well be the *Odes* and for

Dewey the history of the labor movements in the United States. In either case, the source or origin of healing ought to have some relation to past practice, for that is the most economical way to promote the sharing of meaning. The past is a reservoir of energy to be deployed in new and effective means. If this is successfully carried out, two qualities are brought to bear on the situation. First, some measure of succession is made available to the community and without that sense of continuity, new ideas have little chance of taking hold. It is the energy projected from past traditions that seals up the gaps separating community values and interests. But such conformation is not enough. The second quality needed to turn a problem into a solution is a felt sense of fit stabilizing the broken harmonies of associated life. Taken together, continuity and appropriateness make up the core of shared participation needed by communities lacking integrated meanings.

Communal culture is the outcome of shared meanings. The values of the past are to be used to adjust the boundaries of situations that have overrun their limits. From this perspective *ren* and the repairing of communal culture form a set of working connections between American and Chinese cultures. The previous use of the term "elegance" may put off readers used to seeing Dewey as the down-to-earth philosopher of the American way. That would be unfortunate, for the term really means finding the right tone, quality, or perspective that would be most effective in a given problematic situation. Its original meaning is very far from some kind of fashion statement. To underscore this side I would like to make a comparison between the three levels of human growth associated with Confucius—*ren*, *junzi*, and *sheng ren*—and the three traditional levels of Western skilled labor: apprentice, journeyman, and master. All along I have been speaking of the need to establish working connections between Confucius and Dewey. It is therefore entirely appropriate that I conclude this study with an analysis of the idea of work. It should help take the preciousness out of elegance and the haughtiness out of the scholar official.

As we move from elegance to labor, it is important to keep in mind the source of human wisdom: experience. Furthermore, we cannot lose sight of the goal of this study: the comparative goodness of both cultures as they pursue their particular *daos*. So whether we are talking about a journeyman or a *junzi*, it is to be kept in mind that both are highly experienced. And whether we speak of the master or the *sheng ren*, we are always talking about the excellent pursuit of the good.

What marks the beginner is a certain obvious clumsiness. There is a lack of skill that shows itself in the ways in which workers get blocked by their own ego. There is no fluid movement and their way is marked by frequent stops and starts. Hesitation and the fear of making mistakes bedevil the beginner. In fact the entire *Analects* can be read as a course for beginners.[16] What the apprentice must work at in moving toward *ren* as a habitual state of being is facility in the arts of communication. Indeed this essay is nothing less than a sustained argument aimed at demonstrating the unity existing between labor and communication. To undertake the task of becoming *ren* demands a long-term apprenticeship to a master. When cultural complexes are the objects of human inquiry, labor means the creation and communication of meaning. Think of the training needed by the Confucian beginner seeking to become *ren*. "Learning" says the Master "is what I have always sought."[17] So also the apprentice must imitate the master so as to take on the accomplishments of the tradition. Such learning also involves transforming this knowledge into effective action in the present. Thus, learning involves becoming aware of the possibilities and relations latent in different situations.[18] Also the apprentice is now charged with the responsibility of using such learning in order to transform the learner's character. The awareness of possibilities is useless if the willingness to act is not present. Learning without action is empty; action without learning is blind. *Ren* is achieved through action and learning. The authoritative person creates responses that rectify situations gone bad. Through this work, creative communication takes place within the members of the group in question. Such is also the case with the apprentice worker. The master sets the apprentice upon projects gone wrong in the workshop. Such attempts to fix what is out of joint are the first step toward learning how to react in situations that demand creative repair jobs. It is not enough that the worker learns the master's principles; they must also be used effectively. Doing and being are brought into harmony. The first steps are clumsy and filled with error but as the apprenticeship proceeds, more and more effective communication takes place between the worker and the project and between the master and the apprentice. Becoming *ren* is not the work of a single day. The fundamental attitude of the apprentice is openness to the values of the master. This is learning that is more than a preoccupation with the acquisition of skills. It involves a deep change in the personality of the apprentice so that the public can have trust in the work of such a person. This is a direct anticipation of the future of the worker, who will eventually be trusted to harmonize some object with its ideal and its actual place. It is learning to become aware of possibilities and relations so as to be able to establish working connections between norms and problematic situations.

Where the apprentice stays in the workshop, as *junzi,* the journeyman takes such learning out on the road. This involves using learning in a variety of circumstances. At this level, direct tests of the arts of communication are a daily matter. What is required is that the journeyman act in an exemplary fashion, one that reflects the training and standards of the master. This is the quality of action expected of the *junzi.* Each situation, problem, issue, and instance of discord offers an opportunity to put into effect the teachings of the master. A *junzi* is in possession of a portable tradition that make it possible to travel with competence through a range of social problems.[19] In our age this would be the job of the public intellectual. Creative communication and intellectual responsibility are major qualities necessary for success in such a role. The *junzi* embodies far more than individual insight into the problems of life and stands as the representative of an entire tradition including both its triumphs and failures. What is crucial is that the *junzi* have the creativity to experiment with various tools within the tradition. This demands knowing what the community can tolerate and what it cannot. Therefore the *junzi* must participate in the shared meanings of associated life that define the values of the members of the community. To participate is to take part in the social structures used to uphold the values of the community. This requires an active, concrete sharing of the symbolic code used by the community. If it is to be effective, this sharing must be deeply experiential. It involves a double stretching of experience. On the one hand, the *junzi* must internalize the presence of the shadow *soma,* or public body of the community. This requires a radical openness to the unfamiliar. On the other hand, the *junzi* must find within the traditions of the master sufficient adaptive flexibility to address what is out of balance in the lives of the *junzi's* fellow human beings. This stretch will succeed or fail according to the talents of the *junzi* and the resources of the tradition:

"How can you be so dense!" replied Confucius. "An exemplary person (*junzi*) defers on matters he does not understand. When names are not used properly, language will not be used effectively; when language is not used effectively, matters will not be taken care of; when the observance of ritual propriety (*li*) and the playing of music do not flourish, the application of laws and punishments will not be on the mark; when the application of laws and punishments is not on the mark, the people will not know what to do with themselves. Thus, when the exemplary person puts a name to something, it can certainly be spoken, and when spoken it can certainly be acted upon. There is nothing careless in the attiitude of the exemplary person toward what is said.[20]

It should now be evident that elegance as a factor in labor is much more than the use of fancy language or ritual niceties. It is directly related to the felt intelligence that lies at the bottom of Dewey's theory of instrumental and consummatory experience. When the *junzi's* influence as an exemplary person is expressed, the community is made to feel the presence of values directly pertinent to the situation at hand. Through this stretching of experience the *junzi* makes palpable to others the felt values of the tradition the *junzi* represents. As an exemplary person, the *junzi* brings home to all involved the importance of acting in a certain way. As a model the *junzi* represents a way or *dao* most effective for bringing about the balance lost in the associated lives of the persons with whom the *junzi* works. This is the true meaning of the union of elegance and work.

Undergirding the work of both apprentice and journeyman is the vision of possibilities granted by the master. Everything depends upon the angle of vision adopted by the worker. Too narrow a vision leads to modes of control that eventually will become resented. Too vague a vision allows the values in the situation to slip away. Too wide a vision can cause the particular values embodied in this situation to be swept up in a generalized abstraction. And too trivial a vision is no help at all. The basic working connection between Dewey and Confucius resides in their mutual emphasis on the importance of an adequate vision of what is possible in a particular situation. Once again recourse to the four norms at play in satisfactory communication and work is helpful: *Integrity, intensity, wholeness*, and *depth*. Each of these norms provides a measure by which limited visions of possibilities can be corrected. The *shengren*, master or sage, is able to deftly use these measures to communicate creative solutions to the problems of life.

It is breadth of vision that allows the *shengren* to play such a decisive role in the affairs of a community. Relevant possibilities appear to the *sheng ren* because of the *sheng ren*'s intimate relation with universal cosmic forces. That is to say, the *sheng ren* possesses a power to see beyond what is merely feasible to what is ideally possible. There is, of course, a touch of the presence of the divine in the work of the *sheng ren* and Confucius himself refused to claim the title.[21] Nevertheless, the work of the sage, though on a much more demanding level, is the same as that of the apprentice and the journeyman: creative communication of norms by which real values can be instituted within the social environment. There is a test for authenticity that runs throughout the *Analects*. It is not explicitly discussed at any length but its underlying presence can be felt in the dialogues between Confucius and his disciples. The test involves detecting the presence of hypocrisy that is the opposite of the act of "living up to one's word." Now living up to one's word (*xin**) is the supreme test of one's capacity to communicate. It is, as previously discussed, a unique source of the cultural creativity required to face up to difficult situations. As Confucius comments on his disciple Yan Hui, "He could go for months without departing from authoritative (*ren*) thoughts and feelings (*xin**); as for the others, only every once in a long while, might authoritative thoughts and feelings make an appearance."[22]

Integrity sums up the qualities needed for achieving excellence in the world of social relations. For the act of living up to one's word involves the integration of the other norms of intensity, wholeness, and depth. When a dynamic unity organizes these qualities so as to fit a particular situation, then elegance in the best sense has been achieved. Hypocrisy destroys the active drive for effective communication that is at the heart of integration. It makes a shambles out of the ends in view of the community. Hypocrisy prevents wholeness because deceit lies at the heart of any attempt to see the situation in all its ramifications. Similarly, hypocrisy tears the heart out of the community and leaves it disillusioned and on the edge of death. Finally, the only intensity in the situation is reserved for the self-interest of the deceiver who turns the community's problems into an opportunity for personal gain. Without integration we are back at the cultural problem that Dewey deplored: *separations*. Brother is divided against brother, sister against sister, family members against each other, and government against the people. Division reigns and hope for honest and effective communication is lost.

Openness is at the heart of effective communication, and hypocrisy closes off its possibility. This failure to respond to the potential goodness residing in a particular situation shuts the door on the meaning of goodness itself. Recall that in the *Republic* Plato is at pains to argue that the goodness of the good consists simply in the fact that it gives.[23] Its chief characteristic is the fact that it is noncontentious and its fundamental gesture is generosity. It does not oppose and it does not insist. It is simply there and available for use. The human task is to gain sight of it. This is why theory and perspective are so important. Reason can put us in a position to catch sight of the good. Force can never take it by storm. What is required for the good life is the power to envision a good way to be. The phenomenology of Plato's cave reveals this basic truth: we are blind until we stand up, turn around, and look in the right direction.

And what do we experience as a result of the *agon* of the cave? It is here that I would insist on the future importance of comparative philosophy. I take the generosity of the good to be similar in both Confucius and Dewey. Goodness is the outcome of finding the right limits to impose on experience. Through such skillful means an appropriate balance is brought to a disordered situation. It is by no means an easy task nor is it a job for the novice. That is why Plato states that "the Good is always the last thing we learn."[24] Authoritative persons, exemplary persons, and sages are always on a *dao* toward the good. And here, where the human mind appears to falter and fall back on old forms of dualism, it is most crucial to search for new forms of creative communication. Our finite, limited intelligence staggers under the weight of this responsibility.

Earlier I hinted at the deep connection between goodness and emptiness. By emptiness I mean that which exists without a selfish center. Given its generosity and noncontentious way of being, the good manifests just such a quality. But what about the fact that the above analysis defines value as form or pattern achieved? How can such limitation produce such goodness?

What brings various forms of the good to expression as particular values achieved is the fact that the forms of limitation selected act as modes of emphasis. Guided by these forms, new ways of feeling strengthen the ways in which social situations are shaped. Thus the ideals we spy out in the flowing, generous emptiness of the good are the bridge between the felt expressions of the finite world and an infinite universe awaiting realization. The way between the ideal and the actual is a double *dao*. On one side there is the actual world seeking value and worth but passing in time; on the other, there are the permanent ideals seeking life and influence but requiring realization in the actual world. The first words of the *dao dejing* are:

> Non-being (*wu*), to name the origin (*shih*)
> Of heaven and earth;
> Being (*yu*), to name (*ming*) the mother of ten thousand things.[25]

From all this we can see the cultural importance of the practice of philosophy. Identifying the right ideals depends on the clarity and openness of our minds. In fact human consciousness is built upon the contrast felt between the ideal and the actual, for the quality of particular ideals determines the clarity of our vision of what is realizable. This is the great secret of Dewey's success as a reformer. It is, I believe, what compelled the Chinese to call him a "Second Confucius." Like Confucius he understood that the ideal and the actual are already present within the human situation. To the degree that we affirm this fact, we can feel more intensely the value of the human condition. Furthermore, to the degree that we refuse to slip back into an easy dualism, to that same degree we feel the fusion of intelligence and feeling that marks great philosophy in its moments of highest attainment.

Transparency is the quality needed to make the ideal actual. One must be able to see through situations and then provide the appropriate limit of adjustment. Too much and the situation is distorted. Murkiness and confusion reign. Too little and the situation remains unchanged. A sense of failure and frustration brood over the social environment. Apathy, anomie, and alienation infect our relationships. Associated living is swallowed up by despair. Cynical rejection of all things political becomes the reigning attitude. Without transparency the people walk away from community life, for their trust in authoritative conduct has been crushed. The qualities that make for excellence are brought about by human action. How else does faith come on the human scene unless we believe? How else does hope appear unless we hope? How else does love show itself unless we love? Action and ideals are always already together. Confucius and Dewey understood their working connections. No more separations.

Epilog

September 11, 2001

As the preface notes, this essay in comparative philosophy began in April 2001 at the height of the Chinese-American dispute over a spy plane. I write this epilog three months after the events of September 11, 2001. Things have changed and become worse. We are at war in a most unusual sense. In the contemporary age war has always been waged among nation-states. It receives its legal sanctions by governments in debate and by formal declarations (though in recent years that has hardly been the case). Still, one could say that even the recent Gulf War stayed within the normal parameters of conventional warfare. At the very least there was a nation we were at war with. Since September 11 we are no longer at war with a state but with a nebulous, unformed, ill-identified entity called "terrorism." In point of fact, as this war has progressed over the last several months, its real nature has gradually revealed itself.[1] We are engaged in a "ghost war." Now at some level ghostly things are spiritual things. Cultural things are also ultimately spiritual things insofar as they deal with values, ideas, and all sorts of immaterial "objects." In this epilog I want to discuss two questions: (1) Just how far can the spiritually destructive side of culture go?; and (2) What must happen to restore balance to culture?

The philosophy of G. W. F. Hegel was one of the most formative influences on John Dewey. In particular, he borrowed from Hegel four central ideas:

1. That the goal of history is increased respect for human beings.

2. That this goal is what we mean by "freedom."

107

3. That securing this freedom resides in building a culture that supports such freedom through its cultural institutions.

4. That there is an organic social bond between human beings such that they owe each other reciprocal respect and recognition.

Taking each of these ideas in turn we can begin to see just what went wrong on September 11, 2001, and just how important a culture dedicated to the building of a social order based on *ren* really is. First, cultures develop and change. This means they are through and through historical. There is no fixed permanent end toward which culture and history inevitably must move. What is concrete, particular, and practical here and now is what we have to work with. Second, that freedom consists in the management of our experience and not simply the satisfaction of our individual needs. This is something the West still needs to learn and as this study has shown, Confucius can be of great assistance in helping us structure our freedom. Third, both Dewey and Confucius insist on the social ground of individual freedom. Good relations with each other arise from the effectiveness of our cultural institutions. Last, the fundamental debt we owe each other is respect built on the fact that we recognize our shared humanity.

Our first question is, just how far wrong can our cultural assumptions and actions go? Hegel has an answer for this in his *Phenomenology of the Spirit*, one of the classic texts of Western philosophy. The sixth chapter of this work deals with the appearance of spirit as a real factor in human history. It concludes with a chilling description of "Absolute Freedom and Absolute Terror." Historically, Hegel is talking about the terror that took place during the French Revolution. But what he says applies just as well to the attack of September 11, 2001. Absolute terror can only take place when absolute freedom is also present. The absoluteness of this kind of freedom resides in its power to absolve itself of all duties to others. With respect and recognition dissolved, there roams an animal that has lost its humanity. With *ren* gone, the name of the beast is "Absolute Terror."

What is most frightening about this beast is its invisibility. First it is here, then it is there. Its strength rides the winds of rumor, blackening anything it touches. There is no way to stop it, for all law has been absolutely abolished. It is without identity because it is responsible to no one. It moves like the Ghost that it really is. Spirit has turned into ghost and the ghost of absolute terror now stalks everyone. Its freedom to strike is without limit, for it knows no boundaries. Culture disappears as soon as our capacity to recognize each other is lost. Hegel tells us that absolute freedom traffics in death as its ultimate product:

> The unique word and deed of absolute freedom is therefore death— more precisely a death that has no inner reach or fulfillment. . . . It is therefore the coldest, dullest death, with no more significance than the chopping off of a cabbage head or a gulp of water.[2]

When death surrounds culture, the factors of growth and development cancel themselves. Nothing arises but the ever present threat of falling under suspicion. Communication is broken and interpretation ceases. All is like the Roman Coliseum—thumbs up or thumbs down.

Our second question is, how does one restore balance to a civilization teetering on the brink of absolute terror? A response has been developed in the pages of this book. Absolute freedom flies in the face of reality. It is a delusion that creates its own illusion. The delusion resides in the idea that one exists alone and that one can survive entirely through one's own efforts and intelligence. The illusion consists in the creation of a worldview that convinces us that this is not only possible but also desirable. Both delusion and illusion are intimately involved in the idea of individualism that is at the heart of contemporary Western culture. This delusional illusion is made concretely present in the free market economic theory that is poised to sweep over the globe. It is the ethical dimension that can restore balance to a civilization threatened by absolute freedom and its companion, absolute terror. Ethics rests on the premise that there is a right way and a wrong way to act. The rightness of an act is determined by the ways in which it fits into a particular situation. Each and every situation has more than one dimension. It never simply involves a single individual. Situations are relational and therefore there is always at least one other within its structure. It is this other that destroys the delusion of absolute freedom. It is also this other that clears away the illusion that we are responsible only to ourselves. We are not alone.

Ethics is the practical science whereby we recognize our mutual and reciprocal relations with each other. Both Confucius and Dewey set this idea at the heart of their philosophy. For Confucius the test of ethics is always social: Never do to another what you would not want done to yourself. The practical way of detecting when this norm has

been transgressed is the presence of hypocrisy. For Dewey the normative measure to be used for ethical judgment is growth, by which he
means an expansion and deepening of the associated relationships
involved in a situation. The practical way of detecting when this norm
has been violated is the simple question, Do my actions contribute to
making the situation more constructive, or do I render it more destructive by my actions? Both norms make explicit the essential social
ground of ethics. Be it the struggle to create *ren* where there was bar-
barism or growth where there was conflict, the ethical vision is rooted
in the same understanding of reality: a counterforce can prevail against
the absolute terror of absolute freedom.

The remedy for arrogance is humility and the cure for hypocrisy
is openness. Both virtues can make for a powerful stance against the
events of September 11, 2001. Surely, there has been and continues to
be an arrogance built into America's global presence. Like Rome, we
are a superpower that can largely obtain what it wants either through
direct military force or economic pressure. But what of the wretched of
the earth who pay the price for such political power brokering? The
viciousness of the attacks on September 11, 2001, is obvious. Ground
Zero is as concrete an image of the chaos wrought by absolute freedom
as we will ever need. Will we seek revenge or justice? If it is simply
revenge, then more destruction will follow.[3] What is required is a wider
vision of the relations that created September 11, 2001. That vision
must include the injustices brought about by our own actions, especially our inability to see the plight of others. Openness is brought
about by transparency and what is obvious is the fact that others—
many, many others—hate what America has done to them. The war
spirit drummed up by the politicians makes this a dangerous thing to
say and an even more dangerous thing to act upon.

But we must be courageous and examine how our conduct has
damaged others. Ethics is grounded in consistency and one of reason's
hallmarks is noncontradiction. An ethics based on reason also needs to
include a certain degree of universality. We lack the intelligence to
foresee all the consequences of our actions, but at least we can envision what will happen to others if we confine our attention to rela-
tively controllable situations. A sense of a control of consequences is
what marks the authoritative person. *Ren* is achieved when the human
being feels competent to judge what is fit for turning situations into
problems that can be solved. There is nothing ethically ultimate about

the free market system and its insistence upon the primacy of individualism, private property, and the continuous growth of profit. Economics is not a theological system. And the estimation of the value of goods and services in terms of dollars is not the only way to esteem the worth of experience.

What is needed for an honest response to September 11, 2001, is a wider moral imagination. The kind of normative thinking that this study encourages is not grounded in rigid ideological principles. Rather what Confucius and Dewey teach us is the importance of finding the right fit between strained relations so that greater balance and growth develop out of conflicted experience. The unstable, the unbalanced, the precarious, and the unsettled are always with us. But absolute terror and the trauma that boils up in its wake need not be. The normative thinking encouraged by Dewey and Confucius is based on helping human beings gain a feel for what fits in a particular situation. The "fitting" is the fair and the just. No one set of principles can determine for all time what is appropriate in a given set of relationships. Ideology freezes imagination to a select set of options. This shrinks our choices and prevents the full growth of the human person. No human being is merely *homo economicus*.

As individuals, we can become authoritative in our human relations. It is also possible for us to aspire to become exemplary in our dealings with others. But such growth would require a massive reconstruction of our cultural institutions. Learning would no longer focus on the acquisition of a set of skills for earning a living. It would have to shift its main aim toward making us sensitive to the width of circumstances that human beings are likely to meet in the course of their lives. The variety and depth of experience would become the curriculum's focus. The capacity to respond with tact and effectiveness to the needs of our neighbors would then become the norm by which to judge the value of education. Just as Confucius reformed the education of his time by insisting on a creative return to the classics, so also our response to September 11, 2001 ought to involve a courageous reexamination of just how far we have drifted from the ideals of our foundations. Are the towers that fell a symbol of the fall of another empire? Rome's might never restored her greatness. Was it not the love of freedom in concert with others that created our country? We have forgotten the last part of our contract with each other: *in concert with others.*

Our two thinkers, Confucius and John Dewey (the "Second Confucius") put the social environment at the forefront of their thought. It is that shared concern that the Chinese sought to highlight and honor in their recognition of Dewey's high contribution to their culture. It is toward healing the gaps in our experience of each other that Dewey devoted the majority of his labors. We can learn from both thinkers. In particular from Confucius we can draw the standard of *ren* as the measure of our willingness to recognize the effects of our actions on others. From Dewey we can learn the lesson of refusing the splits in experience that drive us away from each other.

But it is one thing to recognize a central problem; it is quite another matter to heal it. What also unites Dewey and Confucius is their stress on the importance of the aesthetic order as the *dao* of recovering wholeness. Feeling and intelligence are required to come together if such a prescription is to be effectively carried out. In calling it "felt intelligence" I have tried to underscore the continuity of this way of being with the past of Chinese culture and American naturalism and pragmatism. But in addition to this sense of solidarity with the past, there is also the enormous responsibility of dealing with our present situation in a creative way. Old solutions relying on military power and political muscle will not succeed. Ghandi and Martin Luther King have already shown us the futility of violence as a way of life. Einstein said that the fourth world war would be fought with rocks. A new *dao* of feeling our way into and through this impasse in our experience is required. Dewey gives us the tool of experimentation; Confucius hands us the instrument of *ren*. What we make of these ideas is entirely up to our own genius and courage.

The last words of the *Analects* are a caution and a challenge:

> The Master said, "Someone who does not understand the propensity of circumstances (*ming*) has no way of becoming an exemplary person (*junzi*); someone who does not understand the observance of ritual propriety (*li*) has no way of knowing where to stand; a person who does not understand words has no way of knowing others."[4]

Notes

Foreword

1. "New Confucianism: A Native Response to Western Philosophy," in *Chinese Political Culture*, edited by Hua Shiping (Armok, NY: M. E. Sharpe, 2001).

2. See *John Dewey and American Democracy* (Ithaca, NY: Cornell University Press, 1991), pp. 147–49.

3. In a manuscript on the history of American philosophy that David Hall was working on before his death he is intent on interpreting Jonathan Edwards as one of the principal architects of the American sensibility. In rehearsing aspects of Edwards's philosophical reflections, Hall begins by claiming that Edwards circumvents the modern problematic of subjectivity and self-consciousness in any of its familiar modes by proposing a model of individuality that is not predicated upon either knowing, acting, or making as subject centered. In fact, the dissolution of the subject is a function of the development in Edwards of a process vision of the world as an alternative to substance modes of thinking. Further, this process philosophy is informed by a dispositional ontology that understands natural and supernatural processes in terms of inclinations or habits of response that are to be normatively understood as inclinations toward or responses to beauty. For Edwards, the communication of beauty is the defining feature of both the divine and human realms. And for Hall, the desubjectification of the individual by appeal to a processive, dispositional ontology, and the movement of beauty and the aesthetic sensibility from the margins to the center qualify Edwards to serve as an original American thinker.

4. John Dewey, *The Middle Works of John Dewey, 1899–1924*. Edited by Jo Ann Boydston. 15 vols. Carbondale, Southern Illinois University Press, 1976–1983. 10:45.

5. John Dewey, *Religious Faith and Democratic Humanism* (New York: Columbia University Press, 1991).

Preface

1. See Roger Ames and Henry Rosemont, *The Analects of Confucius* (New York: Ballantine, 1999), p. 314, where the issue of method is decided in favor of using the method of taking "the key twenty-plus terms in the Chinese lexicon of philosophical import, provide initial glosses, and thereafter merely transliterate them." This groundbreaking translation ought to be considered the canonical text for generations to come. Hereafter cited as *Analects*.

2. Even though it is central to Dewey's philosophy I do not deal with democracy. That task has already been done by David Hall and Roger Ames. See their *Democracy of the Dead* (Chicago: Open Court, 1999) for a comparative study of the place of democracy in the thought of Confucius and Dewey.

Chapter 1

1. See Steven Rockefeller, *John Dewey, Religious Faith and Democratic Humanism* (New York: Columbia University Press, 1991). Rockefeller's work is the best source for tying together the biographical moments that give rise to important aspects of Dewey's philosophy.

2. John Dewey, "The Need for a Recovery of Philosophy," in *The Essential Dewey*, vol. 1 (Bloomington: Indiana University Press, 1998), p. 49. Henceforth cited as *ED*.

3. John Dewey, "Qualitative Thought," in *ED*, vol. I, p. 205. Where Dewey uses the term, "qualitative" (and all its cognates) I substitute "value" since it seems more suitable for contemporary discussions.

4. John Dewey, "The Need for a Recovery in Philosophy," in *ED*, vol. I, p. 49.

5. John Dewey, *Art as Experience* (New York: Capricorn, 1958), p. 169.

6. See the last chapter of *Experience and Nature*, "Existence, Value and Criticism," for Dewey's classic discussion of the public role of philosophy as a cultural force.

7. This is the title of the justly famous first chapter of Dewey's masterpiece, *Art as Experience*.

8. See my two volumes, *Nature: An Environmental Cosmology* (1997) and *City: An Urban Cosmology* (1999), both published by State University of New York Press, for a thorough discussion of this way of thinking.

9. See David Hall and Roger Ames, *Thinking Through Confucius* (Albany: State University of New York Press, 1987), pp. 298–304, for a compre-

hensive presentation of this important dimension of Chinese thought. Alternative interpretations of the Confucian tradition are to be found in Robert Neville, *Boston Confucianism* (Albany: State University of New York Press, 2001); Chung-ying Cheng, *New Dimensions of Confucian and Neo-Confucian Philosophy* (Albany: State University of New York Press, 1991); Tu Wei- Ming, *Confucian Thought: Selfhood as Creative Transformation* (Albany: State University of New York Press, 1985); and Herbert Fingarette, *Confucius: The Secular as Sacred* (New York: Harper Torchbooks, 1972). A valuable collection of essays is to be found in Robert Allinson, ed., *Understanding the Chinese Mind* (Hong Kong: Oxford University Press, 1989).

10. All translations from the *Analects* are taken from *The Analects of Confucius: A Philosophical Translation*, translation and introduction by Roger T. Ames and Henry Rosemont, Jr. (New York: Ballantine, 1998). All citations are to chapter and paragraph. Other valuable translation include D. C. Lau, (New York: Penguin, 1979); and Arthur Waley, *The Analects of Confucius* (New York, Vintage, 1989).

11. *Analects* 2.4.

12. *Analects* 8.13.

13. *Analects* 14.32.

14. *Analects* 4.15

15. *Analects* 2.1.

16. See John Riker, *Human Excellence and An Ecological Conception of the Psyche* (Albany: State University of New York Press, 1991) for a valuable and novel discussion of this theme. See also my *Nature* for a metaphysical argument that this is the correct and lasting way to view the problem of the individual and the others.

17. *Analects* 2.4.

18. *Analects* 12.10.

19. *Analects* 19.11.

20. *Analects* 7.3.

21. *Analects*, p. 48.

22. *Analects* 4.1.

23. *Analects* 4.2.

24. *Analects* 4.6.

25. *Analects*, 15.5. South is the direction from whence growth arrives.

Chapter 2

1. See my *Nature* and *The City* for extended discussions of this way of understanding the union between the felt and the understood.

2. *ED*, vol. 1, p. 147.

3. *ED*, vol. 2, p. 171, Dewey's emphasis.
4. *ED*, vol. 1, p. 297.
5. *ED*, vol. 1, p. 400.
6. See the important work of John J. McDermott, who more than any other philosopher has laid open this dimension of the American experience. See especially his *Streams of Experience* (New York: New York University Press, 1976) and his illuminating introduction to his edited work, *The Philosophy of John Dewey* (Chicago: University of Chicago Press, 1981).
7. The best expositions of Dewey's metaphysics are to be found in Raymond Boisvert, *Dewey's Metaphysics* (New York: Fordham University Press, 1988); James Campbell, *Understanding John Dewey* (Chicago: Open Court, 1995); and Thomas Alexander, *John Dewey's Theory of Art, Experience and Nature: The Horizons of Feeling* (Albany: State University of New York Press, 1987).
8. John Dewey, *The Latter Works of John Dewey, 1925–1953*, vol. 1, p. 198.
9. See Grange, *Nature* chapter 12, "Foundational Ecology."
10. *Li* is a complex notion. In a personal letter to Robert Neville, Chung-ying Cheng lists some seven different meanings. For our purposes the most salient one is: "*Li* is a cultural form (*wen* or "polish") which preserves human values as well as ideal values in man." See Robert Neville, *Normative Cultures* (Albany: State University of New York Press, 1995), p. 165.
11. *Analects*, p. 51.
12. Ibid.
13. *Analects* 12.1.
14. *Analects* 9.4.
15. *Analects* 7.3.
16. *Analects* 4.10.
17. *Analects*, p. 55.
18. *Analects* 9.8.
19. For example,see Warrren Frisina, *The Unity of Thought and Action* (Albany: State University of New York Press, 2002).
20. See Chu Hsi, "First Letter to the Gentlemen of Hunan on Equilibrium and Harmony," in *A Source Book in Chinese Philosophy*, edited by Wing-Tsit Chan (Princeton: Princeton University Press, 1963), pp. 600–602; and Wang-yang Ming, "Instructions for Practical Living," *ibid.*, pp. 667–690.
21. *Analects*, p. 174.

Chapter 3

1. See Hall and Ames, *Thinking Through Confucius* (Albany: State University of New York Press, 1987), pp. 237 ff.

2. See Antonio Damasio, *The Feeling of What Happens* (New York: Harcourt, 1999) for a neurological account of how the human self arises from its ocean of feelings.

3. See Hall and Ames, *The Democracy of the Dead* (Chicago: Open Court, 1999) for a detailed account of the possibilities of democratic government in contemporary China.

4. John Dewey, *The Public and Its Problems* (New York: Henry Holt, 1927), pp. 154–155.

5. John Dewey, *Reconstruction in Philosophy* (Boston: Beacon Press, 1957), p. 118.

6. See Robert Neville, *Recovery of the Measure* (Albany: State University of New York Press, 1989), pp. 57 ff.

7. *Analects* 1.12.

8. Hall and Ames, *Thinking Through Confucius* (Albany: State University of New Press, 1987), pp. 237 ff.

9. *Analects* 1.13.

10. *Analects* 6.7.

11. *Analects* 12.19.

12. *Analects* 13.23.

13. *Analects* 4.18.

14. *Analects* 5.16.

15. *Analects* 6.27.

16. Ames and Rosemont, *The Analects of Confucius*, p. 62. Robert Neville takes exception to their understanding of *tian* (heaven) as something without transcendental meaning. See his *Boston Confucianism* (Albany: State University of New York Press, 2000). This is an issue that needs further debate if global philosophy is to become a truly planetary integrative force.

Chapter 4

1. See Robert Neville, *Boston Confucianism* (Albany: State University of New York Press, 2000). In this company belong the father of the movement, A. C. Graham, along with Chung-ying Cheng, David Dilworth, Chad Hansen, Michael La Fargue, Gerald Larsen, and Steve Odin, to name but a few.

2. Alfred North Whitehead, *Modes of Thought* (New York: Free Press, 1968) p. 1. Italics are Whitehead's.

3. These qualities are borrowed from Robert Neville's essay in *The Recovery of Philosophy in America*, edited by Thomas Kasulis and Robert Neville (Albany: State University of New York Press, 1997) p. 255.

4. John Dewey, *Art As Experience* (New York: Capricorn, 1934), pp. 17–18.
5. See Ames, *Analects*, p. 51.
6. See Michael Eldridge, *Transforming Experience* (Nashville: Vanderbilt University Press, 1998).
7. See David Hall and Roger Ames, *Thinking Through Confucius* (Albany: The State University of New York Press, 1987).
8. *Analects* 8.2.
9. See Roger Ames, *Sun Tzu: The Art of Warfare* (New York: Ballantine Books, 1993), pp. 62.
10. See Ames, *Analects*, pp. 48–50.
11. John Dewey,*The Public and Its Problems* (New York: Henry Holt, 1927), p. 183.
12. Roger Ames, *Sun Pin: The Art of Warfare* (New York: Ballantine Books, 1996), p. 107.
13. See Joseph Grange, *Nature: An Environmental Cosmology* (Albany: State University of New York Press, 1997).
14. *Analects* 11.16.
15. Robert Neville, *The Cosmology of Freedom*, new edition (Albany: State University of New York Press, 1995), p. 71. Author's emphases.
16. Confucius does identify a class of learners that closely resembles the position of apprentice. See Ames and Rosemont, *Analects*, pp. 60 ff.
17. *Analects* 1.1.
18. See David Hall and Roger Ames,*ThinkingThrough Confucius*, p. 30ff., for a detailed discussion of the concept of learning.
19. *The Search for a Portable Tradition* is the subtitle of Robert Neville's *Boston Confucianism*.
20. *Analects* 13.3.
21. See Ames and Rosemont, *Analects*, p. 62 ff.
22. *Analects* 6.7.
23. *Republic*, book VII.
24. *Ibid.*
25. Mary Ellen Chen, translator, *The Tao Te Ching* (New York: Paragon House, 1989), p. 51.

Epilog

1. Actually, as I prepare this manuscript for the publisher, the war in Iraq is being waged. It, too, barely qualifies as a war. It lacks international sanction and there is no contest between the American forces and the Iraqi military. Some wag has said, "It is like the New York Yankees playing Chuck's Variety." He who owns the dictionary owns the world even when it comes to war.

2. G. W. F. Hegel, *Spirit, Chapter Six of Hegel's Phenomenology of Spirit*, edited by Daniel E. Shannon (Indianapolis: Hackett Publishing, 2001), p. 108. The reference to the cabbage refers to the guillotine.
3. This is why the proclamation of "shock and awe" during the war in Iraq is so disturbing. The way in which the media culture snapped up the phrase was chilling; it was lovingly caressed.
4. *Analects* 20.3.

Selected Bibliography

The literature by and about Confucius and Dewey is extensive. This brief bibliography is intended to help the reader find a way into both thinkers. It is meant to be a helpful introduction rather than an exhaustive scholarly listing.

Confucius

Ames, Roger, and Henry Rosemont, translators. *The Analects of Confucius: A Philosophical Translation*. New York: Ballantine Books, 1998.

Lau, D. C. *The Analects of Confucius*. New York: Penguin, 1979.

Waley, Arthur. *The Analects of Confucius*. New York: Vintage, 1989.

Selected Books and Essays

Allinson, Robert, ed. *Understanding the Chinese Mind*. Hong Kong: Oxford University Press, 1989.

Ames, Roger. *The Art of Rulership: A Study of Chinese Political Thought*. Albany: State University of New York Press, 1993.

———. *Sun-Tzu: The Art of Warfare*. New York: Ballantine, 1993.

———. *Sun Pin: The Art of Warfare*. New York: Ballantine Books, 1996.

Berthrong, John. *Transformations of the Confucian Way*. Boulder, Colo.: Westview Press, 1994.

Blumenberg, Hans. *The Legitimacy of the Modern Age*. Cambridge: MIT Press, 1983.

———. *Work on Myth*. Cambridge: MIT Press, 1985.

Chan, Wing-Tsit, ed. *A Source Book in Chinese Philosophy*. Princeton: Princeton University Press, 1963.

Chen, Mary Ellen, trans. *The Tao Te Ching*. New York: Paragon House, 1989.

Cheng, Chung-ying. *New Dimensions of Confucian and Neo-Confucian Philosophy*. Albany: State University of New York Press, 1991.

Ching, Julia. *To Acquire Wisdom: The Way of Wang Yang-Ming*. New York: Columbia University Press, 1976.

Cua, Anthony. *The Unity of Knowledge and Action*. Honolulu: University of Hawaii Press, 1982.

de Bary, William. *Sources of Chinese Culture*. New York: Columbia University Press, 1960.

———. *The Trouble with Confucianism*. Cambridge: Harvard University Press, 1991.

Dilworth, David. *Philosophy in World-Perspective: A Comparative Hermeneutic of the Major Theories*. New Haven: Yale University Press, 1989.

Eno, Robert. *The Confucian Creation of Heaven: Philosophy and the Defense of Religious Mastery*. Albany: State University of New York Press, 1990.

Fingarette, Herbert. *Confucius: The Secular as the Sacred*. New York: Harper, 1972.

Graham, A. C. *Disputers of the Tao*. La Salle, Illinois: Open Court, 1989.

———. *Studies in Chinese Philosophy and Philosophical Literature*. Albany: State University of New York Press, 1990.

Granet, Marcel. *La pensée chinoise*. Paris: Editions Albin Michel, 1950.

Henderson, John B. *The Development and Decline of Chinese Cosmology*. New York: Columbia University Press, 1984.

Hall, David. *Eros and Irony*. Albany: State University of New York Press, 1982.

———. *Uncertain Phoenix*. New York: Fordham University Press, 1982.

Hall, David L.and Roger T. Ames. *Thinking through Confucius*. Albany: State University of New York Press, 1987.

———. *Anticipating China*. Albany: State University of New York Press, 1995.

———. *Thinking from the Han*. Albany: State University of New York Press, 1998.

———. *The Democracy of the Dead*. Chicago: Open Court, 1999.

Hansen, Chad. *Language and Logic in Ancient China*. Ann Arbor: University of Michigan Press, 1983.

———. *A Daoist Theory of Chinese Thought*. New York: Oxford University Press, 1992.

Ivanhoe, Philip. *Confucian Moral Self-Cultivation*. New York: Peter Lang, 1990.

———. *Ethics in the Confucian Tradition: The Thought of Mencius and Wang-yang Ming*. Atlanta: Scholars Press, 1990.

Kaptchuk, Ted. *The Web That Has No Weaver*. New York: Congdon and Weed, 1983.

Kohn, Livia. *Taoist Mystical Philosophy: The Scripture of Western Ascension.* Albany: State University of New York Press, 1991.

———. *The Taoist Experience: An Anthology.* Albany: State University of New York Press, 1993.

LaFargue, Michael. *The Tao of the Tao Te Ching.* Albany: State University of New York Press, 1992.

———. *Tao and Method.* Albany: State University of New York Press, 1994.

Larson, Gerald, and Eliot Deutsch, eds. *Interpreting Across Boundaries: New Essays in Comparative Philosophy.* Princeton: Princeton Univeristy Press, 1988.

Leibniz, Gottfried Wilhelm. *Writings on China.* Translated by Cook and Rosemont. LaSalle, Illinois: Open Court, 1994.

Louie, Kam. *Critiques of Confucius in Contemporary China.* Hong Kong: Chinese University Press, 1980.

Machle, Edward J. *Nature and Heaven in the Xunxi: A Study of the Tian Lun.* Albany: State University of New York Press, 1993.

Major, John S. *Heaven and Earth in Early Han Thought: Chapters Three, Four, and Five of the Huiananzi.* Albany: State University of New York Press, 1993.

Mungello, David E. *Leibniz and Confucius: The Search for Accord.* Honolulu: University of Hawaii Press, 1977.

Munro, Donald J. *Concept of Man in Contemporary China.* Ann Arbor: University of Michigan Press, 1979.

———. *Individualism and Holism: Studies in Confucian and Taoist Values.* Ann Arbor: University of Michigan Press, 1985.

Needham, Joseph. *Science and Civilization in China.* Vol. 2. Cambridge: Cambridge University Press, 1956.

Neville, Robert Cummings. *Boston Confucianism.* Albany: State University of New York Press, 2000.

———. *The Cosmology of Freedom.* Albany: The State University of New York Press, 1995.

Nivinson, David S. *The Ways of Confucianism: Investigations in Chinese Philosophy.* Edited by Bryan W. Van Norden. LaSalle, Illinois: Open Court, 1996.

Odin, Steve. *The Social Self in Zen and American Pragmatism.* Albany: State University of New York Press, 1996.

Ong, Walter. *Orality and Literacy: The Technologizing of the Word.* London: Methuen, 1982.

Rosemont, Henry, Jr. *Explorations in Early Chinese Cosmology.* Chico, Calif.: Scholars Press, 1976.

———. *Chinese Texts and Philosophical Contexts.* LaSalle, Illinois: Open Court, 1991.

Rosemont, Henry, Jr., and Benjamin Schwartz. "Studies in Classical Chinese Thought." *Journal of the American Academy of Religion.* Thematic issue vol. 47, no. 3 (1979).

Rubin, Vitaly. *Individual and State in Ancient China.* Trans. by S. Levine. New York: Columbia University Press, 1976.

Said, Edward. *Orientalism.* New York: Random House, 1978.

Schwartz, Benjamin I. *The World of Thought in Ancient China.* Cambridge: Harvard University Press, 1985.

Spence, Jonathan. *The Memory Palace of Matteo Ricci.* New York: Penguin Books, 1983.

Terrill. Ed. *The China Difference.* New York: Harper & Row, 1979.

Tu Wei-Ming. *Way, Learning and Politics: Essays on the Confucian Intellectual.* Albany: State University of New York Press, 1993.

———. *Centrality and Communality: An Essay on Confucian Religiousness.* Albany: State University of New York Press, 1989.

———. *Confucian Thought: Selfhood as Creative Transformation.* Albany: State University of New York Press, 1985.

Tucker, Mary Evelyn. *Confucianism and Ecology: The Interrelation of Heaven and Earth.* Ed. John Berthrong. Cambridge: Center for World Religions, Harvard University, 1998.

Wang-yang Ming. *Instructions for Practical Living and Other Neo-Confucian Writings.* Translated by Wing Tsit Chan. New York: Columbia University Press, 1963.

Wilhelm, Helmut. *Constancy and Change: Eight Lectures on the I Ching.* Translated by Cary Barnes. Princeton, NJ: Princeton University Press, 1979.

Wu, Kuangming. *The Butterfly as Companion: Meditation on the First Three Chapters of the* Chuang Tzu. Albany: State University of New York Press, 1990.

Yearley, Lee. *Mencius and Aquinas: Theories of Virtue and Conceptions of Courage.* Albany: State University of New York Press, 1990.

Yu, Pauline. *The Reading of Imagery in the Chinese Poetic Tradition.* Princeton, NJ: Princeton University Press, 1987.

Books by John Dewey

The Early Works of John Dewey, 1882–1898. Edited by Jo Ann Boydston. 15 vols. Carbondale: Southern Illinois University Press, 1969–1972.

The Middle Works of John Dewey, 1899–1924. Edited by Jo Ann Boydston. 15 vols. Carbondale: Southern Illinois University Press, 1976–1983.

The Later Works of John Dewey, 1925–1953. Edited by Jo Ann Boydston. 17 vols. Carbondale: Southern Illinois University Press, 1981–1990.

The Philosophy of John Dewey. Edited by John J. McDermott. Chicago: University of Chicago Press, 1981.

The Essential Dewey. Edited by Larry A. Hickman and Thomas Alexander. 2 Vols. Bloomington: Indiana University Press, 1998.

Dewey, John. *The Public and Its Problems*. New York: Henry Holt, 1927.

———. *Experience and Nature*. 2nd ed. Chicago: Open Court, 1929.

———. *Reconstruction in Philosophy*. Boston: Beacon Press, 1957.

———. *Art as Experience*. New York: Capricorn, 1958.

Selected Books and Essays

Alexander, Thomas. *John Dewey's Theory of Art, Experience and Nature: The Horizons of Feeling*. Albany: State University of New York Press, 1987.

Boisvert, Raymond D. *John Dewey: Rethinking our Time*. Albany: State University of New York Press, 1997.

———. *Dewey's Metaphysics*. New York: Fordham University Press, 1988.

Campbell, James. *Understanding John Dewey*. Chicago: Open Court, 1995.

———. *The Community Reconstructs: The Meaning of Pragmatic Social Thought*. Champaign: University of Illinois Press, 1992.

Coughlin, Neil. *Young John Dewey: An Essay in American Intellectual History*. Chicago: University of Chicago press, 1975.

Damasio, Antonio. *The Feeling of What Happens*. New York: Harcourt, 1999.

Dykhuizen, George. *The Life and Mind of John Dewey*. Carbondale: Southern Illinois University Press, 1973.

Eldridge, Michael. *Transforming Experience*. Nashville: Vanderbilt University Press, 1998.

Feffer, Andrew. *The Chicago Pragmatists and American Pragmatism*. Ithaca, NY: Cornell University Press, 1993.

Frisina, Warren. *The Unity of Thought and Action*. Albany: State University of New York Press, 2002.

Geertz, Clifford. *The Interpretation of Cultures*. New York: Basic Books, 1973.

Gouinlock, James. *John Dewey's Philosophy of Value*. New York: Humanities Press, 1972.

Grange, Joseph. *Nature: An Environmental Cosmology*. Albany: State University of New York Press, 1997.

———. *The City: An Urban Cosmology*. Albany: State University of New York Press, 1999.

Hart, Richard, and Douglas Anderson, ed. *Philosophy in Experience*. New York: Fordham University Press, 1997.

Haskins, Casey and David Seiple. *Dewey Reconfigured*. Albany: State University of New York Press, 1999.

Hegel, G. W. F. *Spirit, Chapter Six of Hegel's Phenomenology of Spirit*. Ed. Daniel Shannon. Indianapolis: Hackett, 2001.

Hickman, Larry A. *John Dewey's Pragmatic Technology*. Bloomington: Indiana University Press, 1990.

———, ed. *Reading Dewey*. Indianapolis: Indiana University Press, 1997.

Hook, Sidney. *John Dewey: An Intellectual Portrait*. Buffalo, New York: Prometheus Books, 1995.

———. *The Metaphysics of Pragmatism*. Buffalo: Prometheus Books, 1995.

Johnson, Mark. *The Body in the Mind: The Bodily Basis of Meaning, Imagination, and Reason*. Chicago: University of Chicago Press, 1987.

Kasulis, Thomas, and Robert Nevlle, eds. *The Recovery of Philosophy in America*. Albany: State University of New York Press, 1997.

Kohn, Livia. *Taoist Mystical Philosophy: The Scripture of Western Ascension*. Albany: State University of New York Press, 1991.

———. *The Taoist Experience: An Anthology*. Albany: State University of New York University, 1993.

Lakoff, George, and Mark Johnson. *Philosophy in the Flesh: The Embodied Mind and its Challenge to Western Thought*. New York: Basic Books, 1999.

Langer, Susanne K. *Philosophy in a New Key*. Cambridge: Harvard University Press, 1984.

———. *Feeling and Form*. New York: Charles Scribner's Sons, 1953.

———. *Mind: An Essay on Human Feeling*. vols. 1, 2, and 3. Baltimore: Johns Hopkins University Press, 1984.

McDermott, John. *Streams of Experience* Amherst: University of Massachusetts Press, 1986.

———. *The Culture of Experience: Philosophical Essays in the American Grain*. New York: New York University Press, 1976.

Mead, George Herbert. *Mind, Self and Society*. Edited by C. Morris. Chicago: University of Chicago Press, 1934.

———. *Philosophy of the Present*. LaSalle, Illinois: Open Court, 1959.

Mills, C. Wright. *The Power Elite*. New York: Columbia University Press, 1956.

Morris, Charles W. *The Pragmatic Movement in American Philosophy*. New York: Braziller, 1970.

Neville, Robert. *The Tao and the Daimon*. Albany: State University of New Press, 1981.

———.*Recovery of the Measure*. Albany: State University of New York Press, 1989

———. *Behind the Masks of God*. Albany: State University of New York Press, 1991.

———. *Normative Cultures*. Albany: State University of New York Press, 1995.

———. *The Truth of Broken Symbols*. Albany: State University of New York Press,1996.

Plato. *The Republic*. translated by H. D. P. Lee. New York, Penguin. 1990.

Reed, Edward. *The Necessity of Experience*. New Haven: Yale University Press, 1996.

Riker, John. *Human Excellence and An Ecological Conception of the Psyche*. Albany: State University of New York Press, 1991.

Rockefeller, Steven C. *John Dewey: Religious Faith and Democratic Humanism*. New York: Columbia University Press, 1991.

Rorty, Richard. *Philosophy and the Mirror of Nature*. Princeton: Princeton University Press, 1979.

———. *Consequences of Pragmatism*. Minneapolis: University of Minnesota Press, 1982.

Ryan, Alan. *John Dewey and the High Tide of American Liberalism*: New York: W. W. Norton, 1995.

Shook, John. *Dewey's Empirical Theory of Knowledge and Reality*. Nashville: Vanderbilt University Press, 2000.

Smith, John. *Purpose and Thought: The Meaning of Pragmatism*. Chicago: University of Chicago Press, 1978.

Stuhr, John. ed. *Philosophy and The Reconstruction of Culture*. Albany: State University of New York Press, 1993.

———. *Genealogical Pragmatism*. Albany: State University of New York Press, 1997.

Tiles, James. *Dewey*. London: Routledge, 1988.

Whitehead, Alfred North. *Symbolism: Its Meaning and Effect*. New York: G. P. Putnam's Sons, 1927/1959.

———. *The Function of Reason*. Boston: Beacon Press, 1958.

———. *Adventures of Ideas*. New York: Free Press, 1967.

———. *Science and the Modern World*. New York: Free Press, 1967.

———. *Modes of Thought*. New York: Free Press, 1968.

Chinese Glossary

dao 道

de 德

he 和

junzi 君子

li 禮

ren 仁

sheng ren 聖人

xin 心

xin* 信

yi 義

zhi 智

Index